PROFIT-SHARING LAUNCH MODEL

A Profit-Aligned Methodology For Marketers And Consultants

Violetta Korovkina

TABLE OF CONTENTS

INTRODUCTION

Why I Wrote This Book

I have always believed that marketing and consulting can be an honest partnership, not just an exchange of time for money. However, the longer I worked in the industry, the clearer it became that specialists take a fixed fee, clients expect miracles, and ultimately, both sides feel that things could have been better.

Meanwhile, there is already a business model that solves this problem: profit sharing. It's used by partners, franchisees, and investors. Yet, for some reason, almost no one talks about it in marketing and consulting, let alone shows how to implement it in real life.

That is why I created the Profit Sharing Launch Model, an adaptation of this concept for marketers, producers, and consultants. It's not just a financial formula. It is a model in which the success of the client and the success of the specialist are one and the same.

I wrote this book to:

- show that specialists have an alternative to hourly or project-based pay;

- teach how to build partnerships where income growth goes hand in hand with results.

- I also wanted to provide a clear, step-by-step methodology that can be implemented immediately.

My goal is to help marketers and consultants stop being mere contractors and start being partners who share tasks and rewards.

My Story: From Corporate Marketing to Profit Sharing in Startups

My marketing career began in 2014. I landed an internship at a large agency, working with global brands like Coca-Cola, Samsung, and Procter & Gamble. It was an immersion in real branding and FMCG strategies, and it made me feel like I was part of something big.

After that, I attended graduate school at Plekhanov Russian University of Economics. I studied at the Faculty of Management and specialized in marketing. I graduated with honors.

My thesis focused on business development strategies abroad, specifically how companies enter international markets and the factors that hinder or help them scale. In hindsight, I see how this topic foreshadowed my real-life experience consulting and working with clients around the world.

Before earning my master's degree, I had already earned a bachelor's degree in analytics and statistics from MESI (the Moscow University of Economics, Statistics, and Informatics). That's where my love for systems, numbers, and logic began.

However, I have always been more interested in small businesses and growth from scratch than in the corporate world. I wanted to understand how to apply "big brand strategies" in a world without multi-million dollar budgets — just one person, their idea, and their desire to grow.

So, I started helping out. First, I helped a friend with her language school. No profit, no model. It was just barter: she gave me a place in

IELTS prep classes, and I helped with marketing. Later, the school started teaching five languages.

Students enrolled, and a team was formed. Of course, it wasn't all my doing, but it was my first real production experience, even if I didn't realize it at the time.

Then, everything started spinning.

One project. Then another. Some people paid; others paid with food.

One café gave me a $50 monthly deposit for promotion. I still remember their pumpkin soup, and how good it felt to be good at something and give something in return, even if it was just a little.

I started a blog, began managing projects, and took courses in social media marketing (SMM). My first regular clients appeared, along with my first paychecks. But it was still the classic model of fixed and hourly rates and freelance projects.

It wasn't until the end of 2019 that I tried the profit-sharing model for the first time.

From that moment on, a lot has changed. I learned how to launch products and share not just money, but also responsibility, risk, and growth.

It was no longer just a deal; it was a partnership.

Then I realized that I wanted to systematize this model.

I wanted to make it understandable. I wanted to make it reproducible. I wanted experts, consultants, and producers to be able to use it.

This book is about just that.

It recounts how my story with the Profit Sharing Model began.

By 2019, I was actively launching my own projects. I had an online Chinese language school in partnership with others, as well as English courses. These were not in the classic school format, but rather intensive courses and groups working with students. I was selling my digital products on Instagram, testing ideas, blogging, and slowly grasping how digital marketing works in reality, not just in books.

Then one day, a friend came to me.

She had a blog and an audience but didn't know how to monetize it. She said:

"You're a marketer. You seem to know everything about this. I'd like to sell something, but I don't know where to start."

At that moment, something clicked. I didn't know what price to charge.

I didn't want to charge just for "one-off advice." So, I said to her,

"Let me help you get started, and you can give me a percentage of your net profit. How about 30%?"

That was the beginning.

We agreed that I would take care of the packaging, marketing, and sales strategy. She would

would handle the product and audience engagement. Everything was new to us, and we had no templates, spreadsheets, or checklists.

But on the first launch, we made about $3,000, and my $1,000 share was confirmation that the model worked.

It was a whole new level of feeling.

I put my all into it, and my results were directly proportional to my investment.

No more, no less. Honestly.

Spoiler alert: A year later, in 2020, I helped the same girl with a new launch.

With my experience and understanding of packaging offers, building funnels, and working with Instagram content, we reached $30,000. My share was $10,000.

In a month. In Russia. This was in a country where the top marketers at agencies were earning $1,500–$2,000 a month at the time.

That's when I realized:

Profit sharing isn't just a model. It's a gateway to a new reality.

Since then, I've launched dozens of products and helped other experts. Every time, I've been convinced.

This model provides equal opportunities.

It divides not only profits, but also responsibility.

It opens the way to significant growth, even if you're starting from scratch.

That's why I created this guide.

To give you the tools you need to enter the world of profit-sharing launches consciously, systematically, and with results.

Why Traditional Models No Longer Work

Business is changing faster than ever today. Social media algorithms change overnight, competitors emerge and vanish in a matter of months, and consumers demand immediate results. In such an environment, fixed payment models create the illusion of stability but actually kill motivation on both sides.

For customers, this means:

- They risk investing money and not seeing growth.

- They lack confidence that the specialist will fight for the best result because payment does not depend on it.

For the specialist, this means:

- Their income is limited by the number of hours or projects they can physically complete.

- Even outstanding results do not bring proportional rewards.

Hourly and fixed contracts were created in an era when marketing was slow, involving placing print ads, planning TV campaigns, and conducting lengthy research. Today, we live in a world where products can be launched in a week, and the results of a campaign can be seen the same day. Old models cannot keep up with the speed of change.

The Profit Sharing Launch Model is more than just a calculation method. It is a principle that unites both parties.

The idea is simple: We share the profits from the launch, so our interests are aligned. If the client earns more, I earn more. If the launch is successful, everyone wins. This transforms the relationship from a "contractor-customer" relationship into a "partner-partner" relationship. What does this give you?

- Maximum involvement of the specialist. I am interested in doing everything to ensure an outstanding result because my income directly depends on it.

- It reduces risk for the client, who pays in proportion to their income rather than a fixed amount in advance for "promises."

- The model encourages long-term relationships, repeat launches, scaling, and product development.

This system works especially well for launching online courses, educational programs, consulting services, and any niche where results can be measured and scaled.

Why am I sharing this methodology

I wrote this book to share my experience and show other marketers, producers, and consultants that

1. You can stop selling your time and start earning based on your results.

2. You can build a scalable career without burning out.

3. You can work with clients as a partner, not a hired gun.

In this book, I will provide a step-by-step system for implementing the Profit Sharing Launch Model.

The business world is changing too quickly for the old rules to apply. It's time to create new rules.

PART 1

THE FOUNDATION OF THE METHODOLOGY

CHAPTER 1

WHAT IS THE PROFIT SHARING MODEL, AND WHY IS IT NECESSARY?

When discussing the profit sharing model in consulting or production, particularly in education and online products, the question often arises: What exactly is it? Indeed, this term is rarely heard in the American context. Here, people talk more about equity, revenue sharing, affiliate marketing, retainers, and flat fees. However, a model in which a consultant or producer joins a project without a fixed fee and receives a percentage of the net profit is still unusual.

That's exactly what I want to change.

I come from a country where launching online products based on a profit-sharing model is common practice. The producer oversees the entire process, from packaging the offer to developing the marketing strategy, and receives a percentage of sales. This model has proven its effectiveness dozens of times. Importantly, it works not just because "that's the way it is," but because it's an effective way to distribute risk and motivation.

Why is this important?

Most experts are unwilling or unable to invest in marketing.

They have knowledge, experience, and energy, but not a team, money for advertising, or an understanding of how to package a product.

On the other hand, consultants and producers don't want to be just "hourly workers." They want to collaborate with someone, share the results, and have the opportunity to earn significantly more if they do everything correctly.

Profit sharing gives them that opportunity.

So, what is this model anyway?

Simply put, you launch a project together, and if it is successful, you divide the profits according to a predetermined proportion.

Some people handle marketing and strategy, while others handle expertise, content, or products. Everyone has their own area of responsibility and share.

It works like this:

- It's a revenue share, but not from turnover; it's from net profit.

- It's a partnership without the legal complexity of equity.

- Investment of time and skills without any upfront money.

Why is this rare in the USA?

Because the established model here is too clear-cut: You're either a freelancer working for a fixed fee, a partner with a share, or you have your own business. Anything in between is difficult to classify.

However, it is precisely in this "gray area" that new formats are born. The Profit Sharing Model is just such a format: clear, flexible, and honest.

In this book, I will explain how it works:

- How this model works in reality (not just on paper).

- How to calculate profits without ruining relationships or mitigating risks

- I will also explain how to create a scalable structure.

If you're an expert looking to grow without a budget, this book is for you.

If you are a consultant who is tired of "hourly" clients, this book is also for you.

Learn how to divide profits fairly.

The most common question I hear when talking about profit sharing is, "How exactly do you divide it?"

"How exactly do you divide it? Who gets how much?"

This is the key point. The whole model is based on trust and mutual benefit. A mistake at the beginning will result in either an argument or someone becoming demotivated.

My basic philosophy is simple.

Your share is equal to your contribution.

Not in hours or "feelings," but in the actual value you bring to the project.

This could be:

- The number of leads you brought in through your marketing

- Responsibility for strategy and launch

- Content preparation

- Homework checks

- Mentoring students

- Risks you take on (e.g., targeting or team expenses).

I call this value-based sharing, which is when a partner's share is commensurate with their contribution to the result. This is not an abstraction. In the following chapters, I will show you:

- How to structure roles

- How to calculate each person's contribution

- How to avoid the feeling of being undervalued

I'll provide a share calculation table that experts use for real launches.

You can adapt it to your situation, whether you're a team of two or four people.

Note: Profit is not turnover, revenue, or "something we earned."

It is the net profit, calculated using a clear formula, after all expenses. We'll get to that a little later.

But remember the main principle now:

Your share should reflect your real value. This is true no matter what your role is. It doesn't matter if you're an expert, producer, marketer, or strategist.

If you determine this in advance, there won't be any conflicts.

What is the profit sharing launch model, and how did it evolve from classic revenue sharing models?

In recent years, the business environment has undergone radical changes. Competition is intensifying, client budgets are shrinking, and the demand for measurable results is growing. Under these conditions, traditional methods of launching projects and products are beginning to falter. Against this backdrop, I developed the Profit Sharing Launch Model — a model for marketers, consultants, and business advisors that aligns the interests of all parties and creates partnerships based on a common goal: profit growth.

From Revenue Sharing to Profit Sharing

Revenue sharing is a well-known format in which participants divide a percentage of the revenue they receive among themselves. For instance, an expert might create a product, while a producer or marketer would receive a fixed share of the sales. This model has been used for many years in various niches, from infobusiness to IT projects.

However, revenue sharing has its limitations.

- It focuses on turnover rather than profit. Partners may chase sales volume without considering profitability.

- They don't account for costs. Even with high sales, partners' actual earnings may be minimal.

- There is a risk of imbalance of interests. For example, one partner may invest more resources than another but receive the same percentage.

My Profit Sharing Launch Model solves these problems. It is based on profit sharing, not just revenue sharing. This changes the approach to launching and makes it fairer and more sustainable.

What changes with the Profit Sharing Launch Model?

1. Transparent Structure:

Before the launch, all parties agree on the expenses and projected profits. This eliminates misunderstandings and allows for the fair distribution of income.

2. Shared Focus on Results:

Partners are interested in more than just high sales; they also focus on optimizing costs to maximize final profits.

3. Balanced contribution:

Contributions are not only considered in terms of sales, but also in terms of strategic contributions such as expertise, marketing resources, contact base, and operational work.

4. Sustainable Partnerships:

Since the model considers the interests of both parties, partnerships become more long-term and strategic.

This is especially important for marketers and consultants.

Marketers and consultants often find themselves in situations where they provide significant value to clients but receive limited compensation, such as a fixed fee or a small percentage of revenue. The Profit Sharing Launch Model allows them to participate in profit sharing and receive compensation that reflects their contribution.

For consultants, this means:

- The ability to scale income without increasing working hours.

- They are incentivized to invest in the client's long-term growth.

- Clear motivation to implement more effective strategies.

For marketers, this means:

- Working in partnership rather than on a contractor-client basis.

- Having a financial interest in results.

- Deeper integration into the client's strategy.

This is where the profit sharing launch model is used.

1. In online product and course launches.

This model is particularly effective in projects where the result depends directly on the team's coordinated work.

- The producer is responsible for organizing the process, launch strategy, and team management

- The expert creates and manages the product

- The marketer is responsible for the traffic acquisition strategy, creative content, analytics, and optimization

- Copywriters, designers, and technical specialists create content and infrastructure

With this approach, all participants receive a share of the profits, so everyone is motivated to perform their role effectively and help their colleagues.

2. This model is suitable for marketing campaigns.

This model is also suitable for individual marketing projects, such as:

- Launching advertising campaigns on social media

- Lead generation for B2B and B2C projects

- Personal brand promotion

When marketers work for a percentage of profits rather than a fixed fee, they are interested in more than just "spending the budget" or generating clicks; they are interested in bringing clients to sales and profits.

3. In consulting and strategic sessions

Consultants can implement this model when:

- Developing a growth strategy

- Optimizing sales or the sales funnel

- Creating a new product line

With profit sharing, you receive compensation not only for your ideas and strategy but also for the end result.

4. This model is applicable to offline businesses.

This model is also applicable to traditional businesses, such as:

- Restaurants and cafés collaborate with marketing agencies

- Beauty studios and fitness clubs can use it when launching promotions and special offers

- Retail stores can use it when introducing new product lines

For instance, a marketing agency could run a campaign for a beauty salon and receive a percentage of the net profit instead of a fixed advertising fee.

5. In startups

Many startups use an equity model or fixed rates initially, but profit sharing can be a flexible alternative:

- It allows you to attract strong specialists without making large initial investments

- It shares risks and benefits among participants

- It builds a team that thinks like co-owners

The profit sharing launch model works because it is based on the principle of mutual interest in the outcome. When all participants are rewarded not for fixed hours or a set of completed tasks, but for profits, the logic of interaction changes entirely.

Performers begin to think like partners, looking for growth opportunities, offering ideas, and going beyond their job descriptions to help achieve the goal. This model fosters transparency and trust because the rules and conditions are known in advance, and everyone understands that their contribution will be evaluated fairly.

This is especially important for startups and new projects where there is potential but initially no large budget. Both sides face reduced risk: The client does not overpay for unproductive work, and the team is confident they will receive their deserved reward if they succeed.

The result is strong team dynamics and flexibility in resource allocation, making the model effective not only for marketing and launches, but also for long-term business partnerships.

CHAPTER 2

COMPARING MODELS

HOURLY PAY, FIXED PRICE, AND PROFIT SHARING LAUNCH MODEL

Classic Payment Models

I n the marketing, consulting, and project launch industries, two models traditionally dominate: hourly pay and fixed rates.

Hourly pay seems logical: the client pays for the specialist's time, and the specialist is paid for every minute worked. However, there are several problems with this model in practice. For clients, it's always a "black box" — it's difficult to understand how effectively time is being used, and there's no direct link between hours worked and results. There is also a limit for contractors: their income is capped by the number of hours they can physically work. Any automation or acceleration of processes leads to a decrease in income. This creates a paradox: The more efficiently a specialist works, the less they earn.

A fixed rate (FIX) is a predetermined amount for a project or package of services. Here, the client has a clear budget, but there are risks. If the tasks become more complex, the budget remains the same. This can lead to a loss of quality or conflicts. In turn, the contractor is motivated to complete the project as quickly as possible, sometimes at the expense of the work's depth. The FIX model has no built-in mechanism linking the contractor's income to the client's success.

The Profit Sharing Launch Model has a fundamental difference.

In the Profit Sharing Launch Model, the focus shifts from time or a fixed amount of work to results. The contractor and client agree on a percentage of the project's generated profit or revenue. This way, both parties are interested in maximizing success; the greater the profit, the greater each party's earnings.

It's not just a financial mechanism; it's a partnership model. It establishes a different level of interaction.

- Rather than thinking about how to "work the hours," the contractor thinks about how to strategically influence the result.

- The client sees the contractor as an ally rather than someone who doesn't care whether the project is successful.

Instead of opposing interests (minimum hours/minimum budget), there is a common goal: growth in performance.

Why is this model convenient for marketers?

Profit sharing gives marketers the opportunity to turn their work into an asset. Rather than selling hours or tasks, marketers "invest" their skills in a project and have the potential to earn a much higher income.

Advantages for marketers:

- No income ceiling. If the campaign takes off, their income grows along with the profits.

- They have the ability to influence strategy. In this model, marketers have more freedom and authority in decision-making because the overall result depends directly on their work.

- Long-term partnerships. Clients are more likely to continue working with you if they see that you only earn money when they succeed.

This model is particularly beneficial for marketers working with launches, funnels, sales growth, and branding — areas where results can be directly linked to revenue and measured.

Why is this approach beneficial for consultants?

For consultants, especially those in business and marketing, profit sharing opens up new possibilities. Instead of providing one-off consultations for a fixed fee, consultants can become strategic partners and earn income from implementing their ideas.

This gives consultants:

- Monetization of expertise, not time. If their recommendations generate a million dollars for the client, the consultant receives a percentage of that million instead of a fixed fee for a few hours of work.

- Deeper involvement. The consultant is interested in more than just giving advice; they want to help implement, test, and improve it so the result is guaranteed.

- Personal brand growth. Successful cases with large profits strengthen your reputation and make it easier to attract new projects.

Classic models fall short.

With hourly and fixed models, there is no direct link between project success and contractor remuneration. This leads to three key problems:

1. Speed. With hourly pay, speed is often not in the contractor's interest. With fixed pay, however, speed can be detrimental to quality. With profit sharing, however, both parties are interested in the optimal combination of speed and quality.

2. Flexibility: Fixed and hourly rates necessitate a precise scope of work, and any modifications necessitate supplementary agreements and budget recalculations. With profit sharing, on-the-fly strategy adjustments can be made without bureaucracy if they lead to increased profits.

3. Motivation: In the classic model, motivation is limited to one's duties; in Profit Sharing, however, motivation depends directly on the result. The better the result, the greater the motivation to continue and intensify efforts.

The Profit Sharing Launch Model aligns the interests of both parties, turning marketers and consultants into business partners. This is financially and psychologically beneficial: it eliminates the feeling that

Someone is "working for someone else." Instead, a common team is formed with a clear goal and transparent reward system.

Classic models will remain on the market because they are suitable for certain tasks, especially when the result is difficult to measure in monetary terms. However, in launches, marketing, and consulting, where profit is the main KPI, the profit sharing model is becoming an increasingly obvious choice.

The hidden economy of trust in the profit-sharing model

In any business model where one party pays and the other provides a service, the question inevitably arises, "Are we fairly sharing the value we create together?" With hourly or fixed-rate payments, this question is hidden behind the numbers in the contract but remains unanswered. The client wonders, "Are we spending too much time on things that don't deliver results?" The contractor wonders, "Are they cutting my budget or preventing me from testing hypotheses just to save money?"

This invisible tension often slows down project development. When the parties think in terms of "minimum investment, maximum benefit," they defend their comfort zones instead of looking for growth opportunities. The client cuts back on testing, and the contractor avoids initiatives requiring extra effort. Ultimately, only the status quo wins — and both parties lose.

The Profit Sharing Model breaks this logic. There is no artificial opposition because everyone is on the same team: if the project grows, everyone's income grows. If it fails, both lose. This format forces you to treat your partner not as a contractor or customer, but as a full-fledged co-author of the final product.

The psychology of trust

Within the profit sharing model, the fear of "overworking" or "giving too much" disappears. Marketers and consultants stop thinking, "I'm paid by the hour, so I only work the hours I'm paid for." Instead, a different logic emerges: "The more I invest, the higher the final profit, and therefore the higher my share."

The entrepreneur or client shifts their focus from "How can we avoid overspending the budget?" to

"How can we work together to maximize profits?" This radically changes the atmosphere within the team.

The economy of flexibility

Traditional models are often limited by a pre-agreed scope of work. Any scaling or additional testing requires renegotiation, resulting in lost time. In profit sharing, however, tests and new hypotheses are not a threat to the budget but rather an opportunity to earn more. This enables faster decision-making and the implementation of actions that would be "frozen" for weeks in traditional schemes.

This is critical in marketing, for example, where trends and advertising opportunities are short-lived and whoever acts first wins the audience. With hourly or fixed rates, such opportunities are often missed because the parties are afraid to exceed the scope of the agreement. With profit sharing, the boundaries shift to where the potential for growth lies.

Effect on Strategy

When both parties are equally interested in profit, priorities are set differently. Projects no longer suffer from excessive bureaucracy.

"fear of change." Decisions are made faster, and the focus is always on delivering results rather than doing things "according to plan."

This is especially important in consulting and marketing, where speed and adaptability are essential for survival. For example, if a competitor has tested a new funnel and started receiving applications, the Profit Sharing team will decide to launch their version the next day. In an hourly model, this process could take months.

This accelerates growth

The speed of response, willingness to test, and lack of barriers to scaling create a cumulative acceleration effect. Each successful hypothesis increases revenue for both parties and boosts their motivation.

In the long term, Profit Sharing works as a closed loop: more initiatives → more tests → higher results → higher trust → more initiatives. Real growth is born in this spiral, which cannot be replicated within the rigid framework of hourly or fixed pay.

CHAPTER 3

THE PRINCIPLES OF THE PROFIT-SHARING MODEL

Wthat do I mean when I say this model should be "win-win"?

It's simple. It should benefit everyone. Not just to the expert you approach with a proposal to launch a product. It should also be beneficial to you, as a producer, consultant, or marketer. Both sides should benefit. At the same time.

Here, it's worth asking yourself a direct question:

- What's in it for me?

- What benefit will the person I work with receive?

For businesses and experts:

- There's no need to pay upfront. There are no marketing, production, or targeting fees. This is especially important in the US, where marketing services are expensive.

- According to Glassdoor and other sources, the average salary of a marketer in the US will be $65,000–$85,000 per year in 2024, and even higher for digital strategists and growth hackers.

- There is always a risk of paying for services without getting results.

A profit-sharing model reduces this risk to almost zero because you only pay when you earn.

As a producer or consultant, you:

- You won't just "work for a fixed fee" like a regular contractor.

- You can significantly increase your income if the project is successful.

- You are fully committed because it's not a time-based project — it's a results-focused partnership.

- Plus, you build a portfolio of successful projects, not just hours worked.

So, what is a win-win in this model?

It's when:

- The expert loses nothing if the launch is unsuccessful.

- Consultants and producers are just as interested in growth as experts.

- Profits are divided proportionally according to contributions, not arbitrarily.

There is transparency in profit calculation.

For the profit-sharing model to work, everything must be agreed upon in advance. This includes how profits are calculated. I'm not just saying this. When I started my first projects, experts would often say to me,

"Why don't you cover the expenses?"

"Okay, I'll take them..."

"We'll figure it out later." And then it starts.

Someone expects $3,000 but gets $700.

Or when you find out that you're splitting the turnover, not the net profit.

Or when the expenses you "verbally agreed on" suddenly disappear.

Therefore:

You must specify:

- What exactly is considered profit?
- Which expenses are included in the calculation?
- Who is responsible for which expenses?
- How are these expenses documented?

From my experience:

I was guilty of not always discussing this. Yes, it affected my income.

For example, when we drove traffic to an expert's Instagram account, the advertising didn't pay off immediately but rather after several months.

Most people don't buy right away. On average, it can take up to six months for someone to become a customer. If we only count the profit for the launch month, some of the advertising costs will be covered by future customers, but only after the profit-sharing window has closed.

Example:

Suppose you invest $1,000 in advertising.

- You agree that $500 goes toward launch expenses and that the remaining $500 is a long-term investment by the expert in their account.

- The net profit is then calculated as follows: Revenue minus $500 minus other expenses.

- You share precisely this profit.

What is this about?

It's about agreements. Words. It's about "speaking up" instead of hoping that "things will somehow work out."

Ideally:

- There is a Google Sheet with a calculation formula.

- Profit = Revenue – Advertising – Contractors – Platform – Commission.

- All expenses are confirmed with screenshots, receipts, and statements.

- A "profit distribution window" is conditionally set, such as 30 days after the start of sales.

If this is not the case, then your model is not transparent. Therefore, it is unstable.

Profit-sharing window (return window):

Another important element of the profit-sharing model is the profit distribution window, also known as the return window.

In other words, it is the period during which you receive your share of the project. Why is this important?

Because we often invest in the launch by preparing content, setting up advertising, doing packaging, and creating buzz.

Then, money may come in not only at the time of sale but also afterwards. Customers may pay extra, come back, or pay in installments.

If you haven't defined the return window, an expert may eventually say, "

"Well, the launch is over. What do you want?"

In reality, though, you're still seeing results from your work.

Here's how it works in practice:

In educational products (course launches, etc.).

You can specify:

"I am participating in the launch, and within 30 days after the start of sales, we will divide the net profit according to the established percentage."

If customers can make additional payments or pay in installments, you can specify this separately.

"I will also receive a percentage of all additional payments received within 45 days of the start date."

For traditional businesses (services, online stores, etc.).

If you are responsible for marketing, website development, strategy, and everything else, it makes sense to set a longer timeframe.

For example:

"I am joining the project for 90 days, and during this time, all profits are considered shared and divided according to the formula."

The main thing is to specify:

- The exact period during which the split is valid.

- What is included in this period (sales, additional payments, upsells, etc.).

- What happens after the specified period ends? Does everything stop, or is a new stage discussed?

This model goes beyond launches.

Incidentally, I used to only see this model with people launching online products, but now I'm seeing profit sharing pop up more and more in traditional businesses.

For example, I have a friend who is building a content lab. She teamed up with a marketing partner.

He is responsible for the entire strategy, content, and social media management. He also helps produce videos, stories, and reels, as well as anything else related to traffic and the funnel.

She is the face of the product and the expert. They agreed on a 50/50 split:

- Her contributions include videos, expertise, and service packaging.

- Her partner contributions include strategy, production, and marketing.

- All sales from channels where the partner is involved are split 50/50.

This story shows that profit sharing is not about a niche, but an approach.

For example, if you help a coffee shop increase its customer traffic, you can take a percentage of its revenue growth.

If you are working with an e-commerce company and its revenue is growing, you can share in that growth rather than in its entire turnover.

For example:

- Before: $10,000 per month

- With you: $15,000 per month.

- You would share the additional $5,000 as a result of your work.

The model is flexible.

The main thing is to agree on what constitutes a result and where the shared profit comes from.

Profit sharing isn't about "splitting it in half" just because "we both tried hard."

Rather, it's about each participant receiving a proportionate share of the profit based on their contributions to the project, such as time, knowledge, skills, resources, teamwork, and risk.

What constitutes a contribution?

It's not just "I did something." It's the value you added to the outcome.

To avoid arguments later, contributions need to be broken down into categories.

What does a profit sharing consultant, producer, or marketer do?

If you work on a profit-sharing model, your contributions may include:

Strategy:

- Developing an overall marketing and launch strategy

- Target audience segmentation and positioning

- Working out the customer journey map/funnel/product line

Content:

- Writing scripts for content (reels, posts, stories, YouTube videos, TikTok videos, etc.).

- Creating a warm-up structure

- Prepare a content plan and work with production.

Sales:

- Setting up the sales department (scripts, CRM, and automation).

- Hiring and training managers

- Conversion tracking

- Personal sales in chat rooms (if included in the task).

PROFIT-SHARING LAUNCH MODEL

Traffic and Analytics:

- Launching ads and setting up accounts.

- Analytics: CAC, ROMI, and LTV

- A/B testing of offers and channels

Organization:

- Interaction with contractors (designers, copywriters, and videographers)

- Monitoring of deadlines and production processes

- Team management: partially

Finance and risk management:

- Investment of own funds (if available).

- Responsibility for results

- What the business/expert does:

Expertise:

- Preparing materials, modules, and video lessons

- Conducting sessions, lessons, and consultations.

- Participate in content creation if you are a project representative.

Operational tasks:

- Processing applications/clients

- Student/client support

- Organizing feedback

Legal and financial aspects:

- Document preparation (contracts, receipts)

- Payment acceptance

- Resolving disputes and legal issues with customers.

Why is this important?

Often, a producer brings in a stream of customers, but then the business doesn't follow through.

They don't respond, provide services, or follow up with customers.

Sales drop to zero. Or returns start coming in. The company's reputation may also suffer. That's why you need to discuss the following before you start:

- Who does what before launch?

- Who is responsible for what during the process?

- Who will handle the results afterward?

Life hack:

I recommend recording each party's contributions in a table. Each block should contain:

- Who is responsible?

- What resources are needed?

- How the contribution will be evaluated.

PART 2

PRACTICAL IMPLEMENTATION
OF THE MODEL

CHAPTER 4

AUDIENCE AUDIT

AUDITING THE AUDIENCE AND PRODUCT

Honestly, I believe understanding your audience is the most important aspect of launching a project. This applies whether we're talking about an online course, a service, a product, or consulting. Without this understanding, we risk wasting time on things that won't produce results.

Why is "30-year-old women" not an audience?

One of the biggest mistakes I see businesses make is describing their target audience with two dry lines like this:

"Women aged 30 who exercise." This is not a description of an audience. These are just words.

They won't help you launch a product and hit your target if you really want to.

We need a deep understanding of the audience.

Who are these people? How do they live? Where do they spend their free time? What concerns them? What are their biggest concerns? What is their biggest dream? What problems and pains really affect them?

These questions are much more important than a general, broad-stroke description. We need details. It's important for us to see the whole person, not just the demographics.

Here's what you need to know about your audience:

- Who do they follow?

- What content they consume

- Where they spend their time (online and offline)

- What they have already purchased, including from competitors

- How they make purchasing decisions

- What is their experience with similar products?

Check if you have a database.

Before planning your launch, it's important to understand if there are already people who support you.

- Does the brand have an Instagram account with followers?

- Do you have an email list or a Telegram channel?

- Have people requested materials from you via email or other means?

My personal lesson is that you can "fall short" without an audit.

Once, I joined a profit-sharing project and trusted an expert. She had already launched a similar product, so I decided the audience would definitely "warm up" again. However, I failed to properly analyze what people needed at that moment.

The result? We sold. It wasn't a loss, but it wasn't a record-breaker either. Instead of the desired $100,000, we made $16,000.

If we had conducted a thorough audit, I'm confident the outcome would've been much better.

Since then, I never start a project without:

- Talk to the audience.

- Understand what they want right now.

- Assess whether there is a chance to bring the product to the desired level.

Before saying "yes" to a profit-sharing project, I check the following:

1. The product: How does it differ from others on the market? What is its USP?

2. Competitors: Who will you have to compete with for attention and money?

3. Past sales: Were there any? How many? When?

4. Ask for real figures and confirmation.

Why is this important?

Because sometimes an expert will say:

"Every launch I do brings in $200–300 thousand!"

But then it turns out that those $200,000 were earned over five years, not from a single launch.

You will only find this out if you ask for proof and document it.

My principle:

No project starts without an audience and product audit. This process saves months of work and shows whether it's worth entering into a partnership.

Tools and techniques for audience auditing:

An audit is not guesswork, but rather fact-based verification of hypotheses.

In my work, I use a combination of approaches from Customer Development (CastDev) and my own proven techniques.

1. In-depth interviews

Nothing can replace live communication.

I select five to ten people from the target audience and talk to them on Zoom or by phone.

The goal is to understand not only what they want but also why.

Tip: Ask open-ended questions rather than "yes or no" questions. Give the person time to think — honest insights often emerge during pauses.

2. Google Forms + follow-up calls

My favorite technique:

- Create a Google form with seven to ten well-thought-out questions ranging from demographic to emotional.

- After receiving the answers, I select several people and call them for an in-depth interview.

- During the calls, I clarify points that the person wrote briefly or vaguely in the form.

This approach provides two layers of data: mass responses and in-depth personal stories.

3. Competitor analysis:

Before launching, I always research who is already working in the niche.

- What they offer (format, price, bonuses, etc.).

- How they manage social media

- What kind of warm-up and funnel do they use?

- I also read customer reviews, especially negative ones, for ready-made insights for your USP.

4. Mini-tests:

Before spending time and money on a full launch, you can test your idea with a mini-test:

- Post an offer on Instagram.

- Create a simple landing page with an application form.

- Mini-webinar or a series of stories with polls

If no one responds to the mini-test, it means either that the offer didn't work or that the audience was chosen incorrectly.

5. Customer Development (CastDev):

The idea behind CastDev is not to come up with ideas for the customer, but rather to ask the customer. One of my favorite books on this topic is Ask Your Mom.

Read it, and you'll understand how to talk to customers to get honest feedback, not just "Yeah, it seems cool."

"Don't ask your mom if your business idea is good — she'll lie to you." — Ask Your Mom

6. How many people should you survey?

The number depends on what you want to test.

- If the audience is small and the product is niche, 10–20 people may be enough to see patterns and responses.

- However, if you are planning a large-scale launch or need accurate forecasts, you should survey hundreds or thousands of people.

My "past life" as an analyst comes into play here — I studied analytics for four years and earned a bachelor's degree in the field.

To me, numbers are the main indicator because numbers don't lie. Emotions can distort perception, but a large sample size won't deceive you.

Conclusion:

Combine different methods.

Google Forms will provide breadth of data, in-depth interviews will provide depth, and mini-tests will measure willingness to pay.

Remember, a quality audit is not just a preparatory stage; it's a filter that can save you months of work and thousands of dollars.

Checklist: Ten questions for an audience audit

Use these questions in in-depth interviews, Google Forms, or on conference calls. They will help you understand not just who your audience is, but also how you can help them and what they are willing to buy.

Block 1: Basic Understanding

1.   Who are you, and what do you do? (Profession, hobbies, lifestyle, and context in which the person exists.)

2.   What goals are you setting for yourself right now? (What does the person want to change or achieve in life and in relation to the product?)

Block 2: Pain and obstacles

3.   What difficulties are you facing on this path? What is getting in the way? What isn't working? What is frustrating you?

4.   What have you already tried to solve this problem? (Free resources, paid courses, advice, YouTube, etc.)

5.   Why do you think those solutions didn't work? (People often know what didn't work for them and what was missing.)

Block 3: Behavior and Preferences

1.   Where do you most often look for information on this topic? (Instagram, TikTok, Google, YouTube, friends, chat rooms, etc.)

2.   Who do you follow and trust in this area? (This will help identify opinion leaders, competitors, and potential partners.)

3.   What content formats do you prefer? (Video, text, webinars, stories, or voice. This influences the choice of launch formats.)

Block 4: Purchasing Behavior

1.   Have you ever paid for a product in this area? (If so, what was it, and why did you decide to purchase it? If not, what stopped you?)

2. What would motivate you to pay for a solution to this problem right now? (Consider factors such as wording, results, deadlines, presentation style, bonuses, and guarantees.)

You can use these questions as is or adapt them to your niche. The main thing is not to be afraid to dig deeper. Your future offer lies in these answers.

CHAPTER 5

OFFER CRAFTING

E verything we did in the first step—auditing the audience and the product—had one key goal: understanding exactly what to offer so the person would say "yes" without hesitation.

An offer is more than just a product description. It's a meaningful package that connects the customer's desires with what you can provide.

It's a mistake I see all the time.

Many businesses and experts start with the opposite:

"I have an eight-module course," or

"I offer two-hour consultations on Zoom."

And that's it. There's no connection to results or understanding of why someone should buy this particular thing.

As a result, the audience hears "just another course" or "just another consultation" and moves on.

This is how I view the offer

I always imagine it as a bridge.

On one side is someone with a problem or goal. On the other side is the result they want.

My task is to build a short, strong, and easy-to-understand bridge.

I want people to see that this path is safe and logical and will lead them where they want to go.

Algorithm for creating an offer:

1. Start with the result, not the format. The client doesn't care if it takes eight weeks or three months, or if it's done online or offline. What matters is that they get what they want in the end.

2. Weave in the language of your audience.Use the data from the audit to formulate the offer with the words your customer uses. Instead of saying, "We'll increase your landing page conversion rate," say, "Your ad will get clicked three times more often."

3. Add social proof: Include case studies, figures, screenshots, and customer stories to show that others have already had success with your product or service.

4. Remove objections in advance. If your audience is afraid that "it won't work," offer a guarantee or support system. If they think it's expensive, show them how much they're losing without this solution.

5. Create a sense of urgency. Limit spots, prices, or deadlines. This is critical in a profit-sharing model because we need quick responses to test our hypothesis.

Example: How to refine an offer.

Weak option:

"SMM course with eight 2-hour modules, priced at $300."

Strong option:

"In eight weeks, you will set up your Instagram so that customers will start coming to you without paid advertising. We will work together through the entire process: from profile packaging to sales automation. Guarantee: If there are no results after two months, we will work with you for an additional month free of charge.

What's the difference? In the first case, the person sees a "course." In the second case, they see a solution to their problem with clear results in a safe format.

My rules for creating an offer:

- Don't write an offer before auditing. It's always a guess.

- Test several versions at once. Sometimes, changing one word can double your conversion rate.

- Keep it simple. The more complex and "clever" your offer sounds, the fewer people will understand it.

   Who it's for: [audience segment]

   What they'll get: [result]

   How long will it take? [Time to achieve]

   In what format? Online or offline with or without support.

   Why now: [Limit, bonus, deadline]

   Proof: [Case study, figures, review]

Important: The offer is live. During the warm-up or sales process, it can be strengthened, refined, and reemphasized. This is normal—we didn't carve it in stone; we're building it together with the market.

Five triggers for a strong offer:

(A checklist to evaluate the effectiveness of your offer.)

1. Tangible benefits:

- A clearly defined, measurable result (e.g., money, time, status, or comfort).

Example: "How to increase sales by 30% in two months" instead of "How to boost marketing."

2. Remove a key fear or barrier.

- This could be a guarantee, insurance, feedback, or a support system that alleviates concerns.

Example: "If you don't make money, we'll give you your money back," or "Thanks to our step-by-step support, you won't be left without results."

3. Limitations:

- Limits on time, number of places, bonuses, or access.

Example: "Only 15 spots available" or "Price valid until Friday."

4. Social proof:

- This includes case studies, reviews, and figures that demonstrate others' success.

Example: "Over 500 graduates found jobs in the U.S. after completing the course."

5. Emotional hook:

- A story, metaphor, or image that evokes an immediate desire.

Example: "This is your ticket to business class," or "Close your laptop at 6 p.m. and spend the evening with your family, not your clients."

Testing hypotheses through mini-launches:

If you have any experience with marketing, you have probably heard of A/B testing.

It's a method where we compare two or more versions of something — such as a headline, price, design, or even an entire product — to see which performs better. The classic scenario is as follows: The audience is divided into several segments, each of which is shown a different version of the offer. We then measure the conversion rate and choose the winner.

Mini-launches work on the same logic, except that we test entire product hypotheses rather than individual elements.

For instance, you might ask yourself, "Does my audience need an online course called 'Abs in 30 Days' or a program called 'Straight Posture in a Month'?" Instead of spending months preparing for a big launch, you can do a quick test:

1. Create an offer.
2. Do a short warm-up for this product.
3. Launch sales not for a month or two, but in just a week.

In the first few days, you'll see which option gets more requests, comments, and payments. This approach saves time and resources while helping you avoid spending six months preparing a product that no one needs.

For example, in the online niche:

A fitness coach launches two mini-products in a row: "Fitness at Home Without Equipment" and "Get Six-Pack Abs by Summer." It turns out that the second one sells three times better, so you should invest in a main launch for that one.

Example from an offline business:

A coffee shop wants to add a new dessert to its menu. Instead of buying a large batch, they create a "dessert of the week" and offer it for a limited time. Sales and reviews will immediately show whether it's worth adding to the permanent menu.

Here's another example from the offline business world using the profit-sharing launch model.

Mini-launches also work well in the offline world, especially if you are a marketer or consultant joining a project using the profit-sharing model.

Imagine that you are working with a coffee shop and decide to test a new product. Rather than buying large quantities of ingredients and making permanent menu changes, you do a test launch — a "drink of the week," for example.

It could be a matcha drink with peach pieces and light cheese foam, for example. As a profit-sharing specialist, your job is to create the product, package the offer, prepare promotional materials, and launch the campaign. You work on the basis of a percentage of sales rather than a fixed fee.

Over the course of a month, you will test the product, track sales, and monitor customer feedback. To generate more interest, you could add a promotional offer such as "buy one drink, get one free" or "20% off when purchased with the dessert of the week."

Based on the test results, the coffee shop will receive statistics and can decide whether to:

- keep the drink on the permanent menu

- refine the recipe or presentation

- remove it if demand is lower than expected

As a profit-sharing marketer, not only will you have tested your hypothesis during this time, but you will also have demonstrated the real value of your work to the owners. This increases the chances of continuing the collaboration with new products and promotions.

Creating a unique selling proposition (USP)

1. What is a USP?

A USP is a short, clear statement explaining why customers should choose you over competitors.

Unlike empty phrases ("We care about everyone"), a good USP makes a specific promise backed by real benefits.

2. Key elements of a strong USP:

1. Be specific. Instead of "quality service," offer "24-hour delivery to any city in the US."

2. Clearly state the benefit to the customer. Focus on what the customer will get, not on you: "Save up to five hours a week on report preparation."

3. How are you different from your competitors? What sets you apart? Technology? Work format? Price? Experience? Results?

4. Evidence: Figures, cases, and facts: "+300% traffic in two months."

5. Simplicity and memorability: One sentence with no complicated terms.

3. Formula for creating a USP:

[What you do] + [For whom] + [Key benefit] + [How you differ].

Example for the Profit-Sharing Launch Model:

"I help experts and businesses launch products in the US without upfront payments. I work on a profit-sharing model that allows them to test their idea and start earning from the very first launch."

4. 4. Examples of weak and strong USPs:

Weak: "We build websites of any complexity."

Strong: "We create online stores that double conversion rates through UX analytics and order automation."

Weak: "We help businesses grow."

Strong: "We launch turnkey online courses that generate $20,000 in revenue within the first month."

5. 5. USP Checklist:

- Is it specific?

- Is it unique?

- Is it clear to the target audience?

- Can it be backed up with facts?

- Can it be summarized in one sentence?

In this chapter, we examined the fundamental building block of any launch—creating an irresistible offer.

A unique selling proposition (USP) is the strategic foundation of your communication. It answers the question, "Why should the customer choose you?" and establishes your uniqueness in the market.

An offer is a concrete, tactical proposal for a sale here and now. It describes the product, price, bonuses, deadlines, and conditions, creating a sense of value and urgency.

How are the USP and the offer related? The offer builds on and reinforces the USP, turning it into a specific commercial proposition.

We examined how to create an offer step by step, from studying your audience and their pain points, to creating triggers that increase interest. We also broke down five triggers for a strong offer and provided practical examples.

We discussed testing hypotheses through mini-launches, which allow you to quickly gauge demand without spending months on development or allocating a large budget to production. This method is suitable for both online and offline businesses, including profit-sharing models.

The main idea of this chapter is that an offer is more than just a product description. It's a carefully calibrated combination of value, uniqueness, conditions, and emotions that compels customers to say "yes" immediately.

CHAPTER 6

ROLE DISTRIBUTION

Role distribution is not a formality; it is the foundation of successful work using the profit sharing model. At this stage, partners develop mutual understanding and establish a solid foundation for future collaboration.

In my experience, this is where conflicts and misunderstandings most often arise. People may initially be inspired by a joint idea, but if responsibilities are not discussed and documented, arguments, mutual claims, and even the dissolution of the partnership can arise within a couple of months. The reason is simple: what is not said is taken for granted.

What is self-evident to one person may be perceived completely differently by another. Anything that is not set out in writing—in a contract, agreement, or even a general working document—does not exist in a legal or business sense.

Why is this particularly important in the profit sharing model?

With this model, you don't just receive a fixed payment for your services; you become a full partner, and your income directly depends on the project's results. Any ambiguity in responsibilities affects not only the work process, but also your income.

When it comes to digital products and online launches, at least three parties are usually involved in a project:

- A marketer or business consultant, who develops and implements a promotional strategy.

- An expert, who creates content, products, or services and represents the brand.

- The business or product owner may be the expert themselves (in the case of an online launch) or a separate person or company (for offline businesses).

In offline projects, such as a coffee shop, spa, or fitness club, roles may overlap. However, it is important to clearly define everything.

Real-life example:

Imagine you are a marketer walking into a coffee shop based on the profit-sharing model. Together with the owner, you decide to test a new product, such as matcha with peach pieces and cheese foam. You could offer a promotion:

"Buy one drink, get one free," and you organize a mailing list, create visuals for social media, and set up the promotion. At the same time, the owner is responsible for:

- The owner is responsible for purchasing the ingredients and training the barista.

- You are responsible for the marketing side of things, from the initial idea to the first sales.

- The outcome of the promotion directly affects your income, so it's important to clearly define your responsibilities and the owner's.

If roles are not clearly defined, you may find yourself in a situation where you think the owner should have taken photos of the drinks, while the owner thinks it's your job.

As a marketer, I always try to take on projects where I can clearly see the connection between the result (money, sales, customers) and my actions. I take responsibility for marketing, sales, creating offers, and working with the audience. However, I also expect other parties to fulfill their part of the task.

A clear division of roles allows for:

- It speeds up launches and avoids unnecessary approvals.

- It reduces stress and conflicts and creates a clear reporting system.

- It creates a clear reporting system and ensures transparency in calculations and profit distribution.

- It ensures transparency in calculations and profit distribution.

1. **Marketing Specialist/Business Consultant**

- Develop a marketing strategy for a specific niche and product.

- Create and test offers, including mini-launches and A/B testing.

- Build sales funnels (online or offline), from landing pages to SMS or email campaigns.

- Set up and run advertising campaigns.

- Analyze metrics and optimize results.

- Prepare content for warm-up and launch.

- In some cases, this includes selecting and coordinating contractors, such as technical specialists, designers, and copywriters.

2. **Expert:**

(relevant for information products, courses, and educational programs).

- Developing the main program or product (content, methodology, and materials).

- Conduct lessons, live streams, consultations, and other expert activities.

- Recording training videos and preparing manuals, assignments, and case studies.

- Responding to customer questions about the product.

- Personal branding and participation in promotions, such as stories, live streams, and interviews.

- Guarantee content quality and relevance.

3. **Business/Classic Business Partner**

(relevant for offline businesses or company owners).

- Providing resources such as premises, equipment, and staff.

- Purchase materials or goods (e.g., ingredients for a new drink).

- Organizing internal work (schedules, cash registers, logistics, and services).

- Fulfilling agreements on marketing campaigns (e.g., discounts, promotions, and bonuses).

- Providing data for analytics (e.g., sales, traffic, and reviews).

- Compliance with deadlines and standards agreed upon with the marketer/consultant.

Do not do someone else's work.

As mentioned above, anything set out in writing is protected. Anything that is not set out in writing does not protect you. Therefore, the first step to avoiding doing someone else's work is clearly defining your responsibilities in a contract or, at the very least, in a working document.

Why is this important?

In the profit sharing model, consultants and marketers often find themselves at the center of all processes. This tempts them to take on extra work, such as writing texts, creating visuals, setting up a CRM system, and closing deals with clients, even if these tasks were not originally part of their job description. The problem is that:

- You waste time on work that is not part of your focus.

- You diminish the value of your role. The client begins to perceive you as a "jack of all trades" rather than a strategic partner.

- You may burn out, getting bogged down in operations instead of developing strategy.

How can you set boundaries?

1) Define your areas of responsibility in advance.

When signing a contract or reaching a verbal agreement, discuss which tasks you will perform and which ones your partner or their team will perform.

2) Create a list of "prohibited tasks."

These are the types of work that you will not take on under any circumstances. Examples include working at the cash register, managing customer chats, physically delivering goods, and video editing.

3) Use the phrase, "This is outside my area of responsibility."

This politely but firmly reminds the client that the proposed work is outside your responsibilities.

4) Offer solutions, but don't take on the work.

If a client needs something you can't do, make recommendations about who to hire, what tools to use, and how to structure the process. But don't become a doer.

Real-life example:

In one project to launch an online course, an expert asked me to check students' homework "in parallel" to "provide feedback from a marketer." At first, this seemed like an extra level of care for the product. However, grading homework is a teaching function, not a marketing function. Had I taken this on, I would have lost hours that I could have spent analyzing the funnel and attracting new students.

Golden rule: Don't do someone else's work, even if you think you can do it faster. Every step you take for a client creates the habit of them passing tasks on to you.

This is why it's important to separate strategy and execution in the Profit Sharing Model.

In the Profit Sharing Model, payment for your work depends on results, which depend on both strategy and execution. However, these two areas require different levels of involvement, competencies, and time.

Strategy has separate value.

In this model, strategy determines the project's overall direction and possible results. If you take on the strategy, you:

- form the basis for the entire project.

- require in-depth analysis and experience.

- it shows your partner that you see the big picture.

How does this affect percentages?

If you are responsible for the strategy, you should receive a higher percentage of the deal than a partner who is only involved in execution or provides a resource, such as an audience or product.

Execution is a separate area of responsibility.

Execution involves implementing the strategy by setting up advertising, managing social media, organizing events, and creating content. In the Profit Sharing Model, it is important to clearly define what you are responsible for in terms of execution.

- What you are responsible for in terms of execution.

- Which tasks remain with the partner or their team?

This affects percentages.

If you take on some of the execution, especially labor-intensive tasks, your share can increase by 5–20%, depending on the amount of work.

It is important to separate

- Transparency: Your partner will understand exactly what they are paying for, and you will avoid situations where they say, "We thought that was included, too."

- Fair Distribution of Income: The greater your area of responsibility and contribution to the result, the higher your share.

- Predictability: You can calculate the workload, time, and resources in advance.

Below are examples of percentage distributions based on roles and workloads for online and offline businesses using the profit sharing model. These figures are not strict standards; you can adapt them to your work format, level of involvement, and agreement with your partner. However, they can serve as guidelines to help you build a fair and transparent income distribution system.

Below is an example of a percentage distribution for online businesses depending on area of responsibility.

Area of Responsibility	What It Includes	Recommended Share
Strategy Only	Analysis, development of a launch plan, creation of offers, and marketing strategy. Execution on the partner's side.	20–30%
Strategy + partial execution	Everything from the previous option plus setup of key tools (funnel, advertising, email/SMS, and content plan), or coordination of contractors.	30–45%
Full cycle: Strategy + execution	Full responsibility for results, including strategy, all marketing tasks, launch, and team and contractor management.	45–60%

Strategy and Execution + Additional resources	Full cycle + Investment of your own money in advertising or provision of own contact base.	50–70%

Tip: When you first start out, you can accept a lower percentage. Then, increase it later if you take on more risk or have proven your effectiveness.

Below is an example of percentage distribution for offline businesses, depending on the area of responsibility.

Area of Responsibility	What It Includes	Recommended Share
Strategy Only	Development of marketing strategy, campaign concepts, and unique offers (e.g., "dessert of the week," "drink of the month") Implementation is the responsibility of the business owner.	10–20%
Strategy + partial implementation	Everything from the previous option plus creation of advertising materials, setup of SMS/email newsletters, assistance with window dressing and launch of a test promotion.	20–35%
Full cycle: Strategy + execution	Full responsibility for results, including concept development, promotions, full marketing support, staff supervision during implementation, and sales analysis.	35%

+ **Strategy Implementation** + **Resource allocation**	Full cycle: Advertising is paid for with own funds, and own customer base is attracted using own promotion channels.	40–60%

Note: In offline businesses, the percentage is often lower than in online launches because the cycle of implementing ideas is longer, and the results depend on many external factors, such as location, seasonality, and staff skills.

How to Build a Team in the Profit Sharing Model

1. Why you need a team

In the profit sharing model, a team does not always consist of ten people. Sometimes it's just two to three key players who cover critical areas: strategy, execution, and operations.

A well-chosen team:

- takes the load off you
- accelerates the implementation of ideas,
- directly impacts profits.

In the Profit Sharing Model, a successful project is built on clearly defined roles, fixed agreements, and transparent communication between all participants. Marketers, experts, and business owners must understand who is responsible for strategy, execution, and resources and management. Anything that is not discussed and recorded in writing is not actually protected and often becomes a source of conflict.

The key principle is to avoid doing someone else's work. This protects you from burnout, helps you stay focused on your area of responsibility, and fosters healthy working relationships. At the same time, it is important to distinguish between strategy and execution. Strategy establishes direction and goals, while execution ensures they are achieved. These tasks require different competencies and can be evaluated differently, including in terms of the percentage of the project they represent.

In the Profit Sharing Model, a team is not necessarily large. It may be a small group of specialists or partners brought together for specific project tasks. The payment format (percentage, fixed, KPI, or a combination) is chosen to motivate participants and ensure the project's finances remain healthy.

The main lesson of this chapter is that transparent agreements established at the outset enable effective work, prevent conflicts, and motivate all participants to achieve mutual success.

2. Who pays the team?

It is important to determine who pays for what at the outset.

In some projects, the client pays part of the team (e.g., technical or product specialists), while the consultant or marketer pays the rest from their share.

In my experience, the project manager or content specialist was often paid from my budget in online launches, for example.

Possible options:

- One party pays for all team roles.

- Split expenses proportionally according to each party's share of the project.

- Paying some roles as a percentage rather than a fixed salary.

3. Team roles:

For the online launch:

- Strategist: Marketer, business consultant, and producer who maintains the big picture and makes key decisions.

- The expert creates the product and content.

- Executors: Copywriter, designer, targetologist, and technical specialist.

- Support: Administrator and account manager.

For offline business:

- Manager.

- Marketer/PR specialist.

- Salespeople/cashiers.

- Baristas, trainers, and craftsmen.

4. Payment formats:

In the Profit Sharing Model, the team can work:

1) Percentage: higher motivation, lower risk for you, and economics that converge on project revenues. For example, a content specialist could receive 10% of your share.

2) Fixed + KPI: guaranteed payment plus bonuses for results.

3) The mixed option provides a fixed rate for stability and a percentage for growth in performance.

5. How to select people:

Selection criteria:

- Experience in the right niche.

- Willingness to work on a percentage or mixed model.

- Ability to take responsibility.

   Tip: Start by assembling a "core" team for key roles. Then, bring in others on an ad hoc basis for specific projects.

6. How to Record Agreements:

The principle is simple: "If it's not written down, it doesn't exist." Include the following in the contract:

- roles and responsibilities

- payment format,

- KPIs,

- deadlines

- conditions for withdrawal from the project.

7. Team management:

- Regular meetings (weekly or every two to three days during active phases).

- A transparent task management system (Trello, Asana, or Notion) is used.

- Quick response to bottlenecks with redistribution of tasks within the team.

CHAPTER 7

FINANCIAL MODEL AND CALCULATIONS

A transparent and pre-agreed financial system is one of the key foundations of working with a profit distribution model. Mistakes at this stage can cost you your partner's trust and even the entire project. Therefore, before we start, we must learn how to calculate and record every figure.

1. Why is this important?

In the profit sharing model, you are not just an executor; you are a partner who shares in the project's financial results. This means your profit depends on how well you plan and track:

- All expenses (both before launch and during the project);

- Revenue and sources of profit.

- The formula for distributing net profit between the parties.

If you neglect any of these aspects, you may find yourself in a situation where the project is profitable, but your earnings are minimal — or vice versa, where expenses "eat up" most of the profits.

2. It is crucial to account for all possible expenses.

The most common mistake in calculations is an incomplete list of expenses. Initially, only obvious expenses seem to exist (e.g., advertising, webinar platform, designer), but in reality, there are always more.

Examples of expense categories:

- Marketing: Advertising (Facebook/Instagram/TikTok Ads), promotion by bloggers, and PR materials.

- Technology: Course platforms, CRM, mailing services, Zoom/StreamYard, and cloud storage.

- Content: Photographer, videographer, editor, copywriter.

- Operational expenses include accounting services, legal support, and payment system commissions.

- Contingencies include force majeure expenses, additional bonuses for participants, and urgent revisions.

Tip: Always set aside 10–15% of your budget as a "safety cushion" for unexpected expenses.

3. Agree on expenses with your partner.

If you are a marketer, consultant, or producer covering part of the expenses, it is important to agree upon this in advance and set it out in writing. Similarly, an expert or business owner should not spend project money without your knowledge.

A good practice is to implement a two-signature rule, whereby any expenditure from the project budget must be confirmed by both parties. This eliminates disputes such as "I didn't know we were spending money on that" or "Why did we buy that?"

4. How to Calculate Profit

To determine how much each participant has earned, you must clearly define the concept of "net profit" for your project.

The basic formula looks like this:

Net profit = Gross income – All expenses

Gross income is the total amount received from customers (including prepayments, full payments, installments, etc.).

All expenses include everything that went into the project, such as advertising, services, contractors, taxes, and commissions.

5. Distribution example

After calculating the net profit, it is divided among the parties as agreed. For example:

Expert: 60%

Marketer/Producer: 40%

These percentages may vary depending on the

- the role and contribution of each partner;

- who invested money in advertising,

- the level of involvement of the parties in operational work

6. Documenting calculations

To avoid conflicts, I recommend the following:

1) Keep a shared Google Sheets table accessible to both parties.

2) Divide the table into tabs for income, expenses, and profit.

3) Update the table weekly or after receiving funds.

4) Keep all receipts, invoices, and work completion reports.

7. Personal experience

In my experience, there was a project where we did not initially specify how to account for discounts and bonuses to customers. As a result, we lost about 8% of our profits because everyone calculated them differently. Since then, I always specify:

- How discounts and bonuses are accounted for.

- How returns are recorded;

- How partial payments are divided.

8. Recommendation

Don't treat calculations as a "formality." They are a tool that protects you and your business partner. Transparency in numbers is the foundation of long-term cooperation.

In the Profit Sharing Model, who pays for what?

One of the key points in the profit sharing model is agreeing on who pays for what. At first, this may seem obvious: "I'm responsible for marketing, and you

You are responsible for the product," but dozens of small and large expenses arise in the process. If these expenses are not discussed in advance, misunderstandings can easily arise, leaving both parties convinced that the other is paying.

I view this format as a temporary partnership in which both parties act as co-founders for the duration of the project. It is important not only to divide areas of responsibility but also to determine how certain tasks will be paid for, whether from personal funds before launch or from total revenue after sales.

PROFIT-SHARING LAUNCH MODEL

In my experience, there have been different options. Sometimes, I took full responsibility for paying my team, such as a project manager or a content specialist working with me on the marketing side. In other projects, the expert and I included these people in the overall budget and paid them from the project's cash flow. In some cases, I paid people a percentage of my share instead of a fixed amount. For instance, the content manager received 10% of my income from the project, which motivated him more than a fixed salary would have. This format also helped with the economics of launches, especially in the beginning when the budget is limited.

Some expenses make sense to assign to each party. The expert usually pays for everything related to creating and packaging the product, such as recording lessons, preparing teaching materials, and curator work. The marketer takes care of everything related to promotion, such as advertising, technical specialists, and designers for marketing materials. There is also a common pool of expenses that we share, such as studio rent, large PR campaigns, and collaborations.

To avoid confusion, it is best to put agreements in writing. This isn't because anyone plans to protect anyone else from dishonesty, but because human memory is selective. A couple of months later, when the project is in its active phase, it's easy to forget who was supposed to pay for a new platform module or an unscheduled photo shoot. I often use a separate sheet in a shared spreadsheet where each expense is listed along with who is paying, the date of the agreement, and the source of payment.

Sometimes, at the beginning, one of the partners invests more. This is normal, but it's worth discussing in advance how this contribution will be compensated. You can agree that the amount will be returned from the first revenue, after which the profit is divided equally. Alternatively, you can consider it an additional contribution and temporarily adjust the distribution percentage.

The main tip is to discuss everything before launching. Even the small details. When selling or actively recruiting participants, you don't want to have to decide who will pay for the target audience or printing handouts for offline events. Clear agreements save you from stress, maintain trust, and help you focus on what's important: the project results.

Here's how to account for contributions and distribute percentages:

When working with a profit-sharing model, remember that you are sharing not only profits but also responsibilities. Contributions to a project can vary. Some people invest money, some invest time, and some bring key resources or connections to the table. All of these are assets, and the percentage distribution is determined based on these assets.

Why contributions need to be recorded:

Partnerships don't fall apart because someone "didn't do their part," but because no one recorded what they were supposed to do. Therefore, the first thing you should do is sit down with your partner and honestly write down the following:

- What are the key areas of responsibility in the project?

- Who is responsible for what?

- How much time and resources are planned for each area?

What is the time contribution as a percentage

Contributions to a project are not just about money. For example, if a marketer spends 40 hours per month on strategy, advertising, and funnels and an expert spends 60 hours on content, lessons, and presentations, their percentage share may be equal or different depending on the agreement.

The important thing to understand is that time is also a valuable asset that should be taken into account, even if it is not paid for directly.

Example:

- Marketer: Strategy, funnels, and ad launch — 40 hours.

- Expert: lesson preparation, filming, and live streaming — 60 hours.

- Total contribution: 100 hours → Marketer: 40%; Expert: 60%.

While these figures do not necessarily correspond exactly to the percentage of profit, they serve as a basis for an honest discussion.

Table of Responsibilities and Contributions

Task / Area of responsibility	Who is responsible	Approximate volume (hours)	Percentage of total time
Strategy and marketing	Marketing specialist	4	40
Content creation	Expert	60	60
Administrative work	Both	10 (5+5)	—
Customer service / support	Expert	20	—

How to Use:

1. Fill out the table at the beginning of the project.

2. Review it every one to two months.

3. If someone's contribution increases significantly, adjust the percentages accordingly.

Combine with financial contributions.

If the project involves monetary investments and time contributions, combine both parameters. For example, an expert may have invested $5,000 and 60 hours, while a marketer may have invested $0 and 40 hours. In this case, you can make each type of contribution equal in weight or prioritize money.

The main rule:

Don't do someone else's work. If you are a marketer, don't take on content creation, sales, or technical support. If you are an expert, don't get involved in advertising or marketing. Everyone should work in their area of expertise as much as possible so that their percentage reflects their main contribution.

Mistakes that cost money

Even with the perfect strategy and a strong team, a project can lose profits due to organizational or communication errors. Below are the most common situations where money is lost and how to avoid them.

1. Unapproved expenses:

A common problem is when project partners incur expenses without discussing them in advance.

For example, a marketer might order a new landing page from a contractor while a different expert pays for video editing in a different style. This results in some of the work being duplicated or not used.

How to avoid this:

- Always record all planned expenses in a shared document or chat channel.

- Any expenditure outside the approved budget should be agreed upon by the other partner first.

2. Lack of a clear financial model:

Without a transparent system for accounting for income and expenses, it is easy to lose control of profits. As a result, some of the money may "disappear" in the form of small payments or unnecessary subscriptions.

How to avoid this:

- At the beginning of the project, create a budget table with a plan/actual breakdown for each expense item.

- Review it at least once a month.

3. Incorrect distribution of percentages:

Sometimes, percentages are fixed without considering the actual contribution. Consequently, one partner may spend twice as much time and resources but receive the same amount as the other partner. This is demotivating and often leads to a breakdown in cooperation.

How to avoid this:

- Specify what the percentage distribution is based on, such as time, money, or resources.

- Regularly review the agreements if the contributions change.

4. Incorrect prioritization of expenses:

Instead of investing in key growth areas such as advertising, product development, and packaging, money is spent on secondary things like excessive decoration, expensive but non-critical services, and unnecessary printed materials.

How to avoid it:

- Divide all expenses into "growth investments" and "secondary expenses."

- Priority funding should be given to the former.

5. Lack of a safety buffer:

Many businesses distribute all profits immediately, forgetting to set aside a reserve for emergencies. When money is suddenly needed for urgent repairs, customer refunds, or an increase in the advertising budget, there is none available.

How to avoid this:

- Include a mandatory reserve of 5–15% of profits in your financial model.

6. "Gray areas" of responsibility:

If responsibility for paying for services, contractors, or customer refunds is unclear, expenses may be duplicated or remain unpaid, damaging the project's reputation.

How to avoid this:

- Specify in the document who pays for what and from which budget.

A financial model is the foundation for transparent relationships between partners and a guarantee that the project will grow steadily rather than "on luck." Clearly defined rules about who pays for what, how contributions are accounted for, and how profits are distributed eliminate potential conflicts, allowing you to focus on development rather than disputes.

The main principle of the profit sharing model is that each partner receives remuneration in proportion to their contribution, whether it be money, time, or resources. This flexibility allows the model to adapt to different work formats, such as online and offline businesses, and remain fair when circumstances change.

For the model to work, it is necessary to:

- All expenses, even the smallest ones, must be taken into account and recorded in a shared document.

- Agree on any expenses outside the budget.

- Have a transparent system for calculating percentages based on actual contributions.

- Avoid mistakes that eat into profits, such as uncoordinated expenses, blurred roles, incorrect spending priorities, and a lack of reserves.

An important point is that a financial model is a living tool. It requires regular review, especially for long-term projects when workloads or priorities change. Checking once a quarter to ensure everything aligns with the current reality protects the project from imbalances and dissatisfaction.

Ultimately, a competent financial model transforms work under the profit sharing model into a partnership where everyone understands the value of their contribution, receives fair compensation, and cares about the overall result. It's not just about money; it's also about trust, responsibility, and strategic thinking. Without these, sustainable growth is impossible.

CHAPTER 8

LEGAL ASPECTS AND AGREEMENTS

Important: Everything in this chapter is based on my personal experience with projects and partnerships. This is not legal advice. Be sure to consult with lawyers and accountants before making decisions about contracts and financial matters.

When joining a project under a profit-sharing model or any other partnership format, you essentially become temporary co-founders. This means that all key agreements—roles, percentages, terms, contributions, and deadlines—must be recorded in writing as well as verbally.

Many people are afraid of paperwork—they say, "We trust each other. Why ruin the relationship with a contract?" However, experience shows that it is precisely the lack of clear documentation that ruins relationships when disputes arise.

Legal documentation is not about mistrust. It's about clarity, respect, and protecting joint efforts.

Why don't verbal agreements work?

- Memory fails. Three months later, you may remember one figure while your partner remembers another.

- Contributions are assessed differently. When a project becomes profitable, each party begins to view their participation differently.

- Circumstances change. Someone may move, change their priorities, or want to leave the project.

- Emotions get in the way. Even a good partner may reconsider their vision under pressure.

Formats for recording agreements

1. Full Contract:

This format is suitable for serious and long-term projects, especially if significant sums are involved or if you are creating a scalable product.

The contract includes all terms and conditions, from roles to profit distribution and intellectual property protection.

2. Memorandum or Letter of Intent:

Used for test or trial launches. A memorandum is easier and faster to prepare but still provides clarity and a basis for a future contract.

3. Fixing in correspondence:

It provides a minimum level of protection. If you are not yet ready to sign a contract, formalize the agreement in an email or messenger and save the screenshots.

However, remember that this is weak protection, especially if a legal dispute arises.

How to correctly record an agreement

1) Define roles and areas of responsibility.

Decide who is responsible for what. For example, the marketer is responsible for strategy and promotion, while the expert is responsible for the product and content, and the manager is responsible for operational tasks.

The more detailed the description, the less likely it is that someone will "meddle" in someone else's work.

2) Define the terms of profit distribution.

Specify the exact percentage, calculation formula, and payment terms.

For example: "The marketer receives 40% of the net profit, paid once a month within five business days after the end of the reporting period."

3) Agree on the contribution of each party.

This includes not only money, but also time, resources, connections, and infrastructure. Specify who contributes what and how much.

4) Establish a procedure for agreeing on expenses.

Even small expenses must be confirmed by both parties, especially in profit-sharing models. This will prevent conflicts.

5) Describe the conditions for withdrawing from the project.

What will happen to profits, assets, the customer base, and product rights if one of the partners wants to leave?

The main goal of the agreement

Not to "trick" your partner or restrict their freedom, but rather to establish transparent and understandable rules. With a contract in place, you can focus on growing and developing the project rather than engaging in endless discussions about who owes what to whom.

What is important to include in a contract for joint ventures and projects?

A partnership agreement is not just a formality; it is the foundation of a long-term, transparent relationship. Without clear rules, it's easy to end up in a situation where the parties' expectations don't align, causing disputes that interfere with business. Whether you are launching an online course, opening a coffee shop, or starting a marketing agency, the key points remain the same.

1. Subject of the agreement:

Define exactly what you are doing together:

- type of activity: selling an educational product, opening an offline location, creating an IT service, manufacturing, etc.

- target audience or market;

- key stages (preparation, launch, operations, and scaling);

- who owns the final product, brand, or trademark?

For an offline business, this could be a joint venture to open a fitness studio where one partner is responsible for the premises and equipment and the other is responsible for the training methodology and customer acquisition.

2. Roles and areas of responsibility:

Clearly define who is responsible for what. This may include:

- Marketing and sales management: promotion strategy, advertising, and PR.

- Operations: personnel management, quality control, and logistics.

- Product/Service: product creation and support, staff training, and customer service.

In my experience, there was a coffee shop where one partner was responsible for marketing and the other was responsible for working with suppliers and staff. Thanks to the agreement, there were no conflicts about who was responsible for what.

3. Financial terms:

In business, it is especially important to specify the following:

- the principle of profit distribution (net profit after all expenses or gross profit);

- frequency of payments;

- who bears what expenses (e.g., rent, purchases, salaries, advertising).

For example, in an offline business, one partner may cover the cost of renting premises and purchasing equipment, while another may cover marketing and HR costs.

4. Contributions of the parties:

Contributions can be financial (money), time-based (work, skills, or connections), or expertise-based.

- Time contributions include the number of hours per week, participation in key processes, and personal presence at the facility or in the project.

- Resources include premises, equipment, software, customer bases, and connections.

In one case involving an offline English school, one partner contributed the premises and furniture, and another contributed the brand, methodology, and teaching staff.

5. Key decisions:

How will you make decisions:

- On major purchases

- Price changes

- Hiring key employees

- Opening new branches or scaling up

The contract can specify a limit above which both parties must agree (e.g., any expense over $1,000).

6. Term of the agreement:

Specify the start and end dates of the agreement, as well as the renewal terms. For businesses, it is especially important to specify what happens to the assets upon termination of the agreement.

7. Termination:

What does the withdrawing partner receive

- Compensation for their share

- The right or prohibition to work in a similar niche;

- Order of transfer of cases.

8. Rights to assets:

Record who owns:

- The brand, domains, social media accounts
- Equipment and real estate
- Equipment and real estate.
- Methods, recipes, and technologies.

9. Confidentiality:

This is especially important for businesses with unique technologies, recipes, or customer bases.

10. Force Majeure:

What to do if one of the partners is temporarily unable to work due to illness, relocation, or a crisis.

How to discuss money without burning bridges

One of the most difficult topics in a partnership is discussing finances. Often, money is the cause of conflict, even if the idea and product are successful. I see three main reasons why partners "burn out" in the process:

1. There are no clear agreements.
2. Too many emotions and assumptions instead of facts.
3. Fear of being seen as "greedy" or, conversely, "taken advantage of."

Because of this, people either avoid talking about money altogether or only start discussing it when a conflict arises, which is often too late and when tensions are running high.

1. **It is important to move conversations about money to a constructive level.**

It's important to agree right away that finances are a working tool, not a personal matter. We don't discuss "who tries harder" or "who is more important," but rather, we talk about numbers, expenses, income, and facts.

In my startups, I often hold "financial planning meetings." Once a week or a month, we meet to discuss numbers only. There is no room for accusations or emotions at these meetings, only reports and plans.

2. **Put agreements in writing.**

Verbal promises are the main cause of disappointment. Even if you think, "We're friends. We understand each other," put it in writing:

- The percentage of profit distribution

- Who is responsible for which expenses

- When and how payments will be made

- What should be done if the project temporarily has no income

In an offline project I led as a consultant, the partners initially decided not to "burden themselves with paperwork." Six months later, they began arguing about who should pay the rent during a month with no sales.

3. **Divide expenses according to a formula, not feelings.**

A clear formula eliminates feelings of unfairness. For example:

- Net profit = Income – Expenses (rent, advertising, salaries, taxes).

- Then, the profit is distributed in an agreed-upon proportion (e.g., 50/50 or 70/30).

Important: If you have different contributions—financial, time, or expertise—the distribution should take everything into account. Sometimes, it is useful to agree from the beginning that one partner will receive a larger percentage for the first few months to compensate for the initial investment.

4. Keep personal and business money separate.

A common mistake is when partners spend project money on personal expenses, thinking they'll "pay it back later." This almost always leads to tension. The best solution is to set up a separate account through which all transactions pass.

5. Discuss unpleasant scenarios in advance.

People are usually happy to discuss how they will divide the profits, but almost no one talks about what will happen if:

- The project temporarily goes into the red
- One of the partners is unable to work for several months
- Unexpected expenses arise

In my experience, including these scenarios in the contract helps the project weather crises much more calmly.

6. Emotional hygiene when talking about money.

Discussions about finances often cause stress, especially if partners have different views on risk, saving, or investing. Here are a few techniques that can help:

- Schedule a separate meeting to discuss finances (not at the end of a hard day)

- Prepare data and calculations in advance rather than discussing things "from memory"

- Agree that if the conversation reaches an impasse, you will take a break and return to the topic later

From my experience, in one project, a partner reacted very emotionally to any decline in profits. We agreed that I would show him quarterly graphs rather than weekly ones so that he could see the big picture instead of focusing on fluctuations. This made it easier to talk.

7. Maintain regular transparency.

Even if you have a contract, mistrust will arise if financial information is kept secret. At least once a month, both parties should have access to the following:

- income and expense reports,

- forecasts for the next period,

- spending plans for advertising, materials, rent, etc.

Ten phrases for gently starting a conversation about money:

1. "Let's discuss how we allocate income and expenses so that we have transparency and peace of mind in the future."

2. "It's important for me to understand how we're going to manage our finances to avoid misunderstandings."

3. "I suggest we agree on payment rules before we start earning money."

4. "How do you envision the fair distribution of profits in our project?"

5. "Let's draw up a table of expenses and income together so that everything is clear."

6. "I want to understand how we will act if there is a month without profit."

7. "Let's put our agreements in writing so that we can refer to them later."

8. "I suggest we have a separate meeting to discuss finances so we don't miss anything."

9. "Let's discuss in advance what we'll do with large, unplanned expenses."

10. "I want us both to feel financially secure. Let's discuss the details."

Mistakes and Failure Stories: What Can Go Wrong Without Legal Protection?

In a business partnership, especially in a profit-sharing model or as a business consultant, everything seems simple as long as the relationship with your partner is good and the project is profitable. However, as soon as a crisis hits, unwritten agreements become risky. Financial losses are not the only risk; your reputation, access to your audience, and even your entire business could be at stake.

A case from my practice:

In one of my projects, an expert and I worked on launching an online product and agreed to distribute profits according to a predetermined percentage. We verbally agreed that all major expenses would be approved together, and that we would share access to key tools. However, at a certain stage, the expert, concerned about the speed of decision-making, began paying for additional services without my knowledge. In turn, I hired contractors for my tasks without prior agreement. This resulted in a fragmented financial picture, and by the end of the month, we had spent nearly twice our planned budget. Had the contract included a clear procedure for approving expenses, this could have been avoided.

Case study from a colleague in the field:

My colleague, a profit-sharing marketer, was in a much tougher situation. She and an expert started a project as partners and split the income in half. No contract was signed; everything was based on trust. At some point, the project took off. One day, however, the expert simply took away all access — from social media accounts to payment systems — and excluded my colleague from the project. Although payments from clients continued to come in, the marketer didn't receive a penny. The reason was simple: legally, he had no rights to the business, and proving his share became virtually impossible.

This is an example of the "we're friends, why do we need a contract" mistake.

Very often, partners say at the beginning, "We're friends. Why do we need a contract?" "We know each other. Why waste time on a contract?" However, experience shows that conflicts between friends can be the most painful. Business is about numbers, processes, and responsibility, not just emotions. A contract doesn't protect you from people, but from circumstances when everyone sees the situation differently.

Mistakes with access and rights

Even if a profit percentage is specified, it's important to specify in the contract who owns the accounts, domains, customer databases, courses, and content. Otherwise, if the partnership ends, one party may be left without the necessary tools, despite having invested considerable effort and money in the project.

The mistake of "gray" accounting

When partners work without a clear financial system and settle accounts verbally or via messenger, there is a high risk of losing income or being unable to defend it legally. Even if you work in a creative field and formalities seem to slow down the process, competent accounting of income and expenses is not bureaucracy; it's your protection.

In conclusion, every time you think, "It's clear," ask yourself, "What if we stop working together tomorrow?" If you don't have a clear, documented plan, then the risk of losing everything is too high.

If you don't have a clear and documented plan, then the risk of losing everything is too great.

How can you avoid these mistakes?

To reduce the risk of financial losses, conflicts, and loss of control over the project, establish a system of agreements at the outset. Below are proven steps to help protect your interests.

1. Sign a contract before starting work.

Do not start a project without putting the terms in writing. Even a simple, one-page agreement creates a legal basis for protecting your rights. Include the following:

- Clear roles and areas of responsibility for each partner;

- The payment procedure and terms;

- Terms of ownership of assets, such as accounts, databases, and courses;

- The procedure for withdrawing from the project and transferring matters should also be specified.

2. Specify intellectual property rights.

Specify who owns the content, training materials, designs, and technical solutions that are created. This is especially important if the project is growing and the investments of the parties involved are uneven.

3. Divide access and make backup copies.

All key access details (social networks, websites, and payment systems) should be stored in an encrypted password manager to which both parties have access. Regularly back up files and customer databases.

4. Record all financial transactions.

Maintain a joint income and expense report that shows the date, amount, and purpose of each payment. This can be done in Google Sheets, which partners can access. This approach eliminates questions about "where the money went" and simplifies profit distribution.

5. Write a "divorce plan."

In the contract, specify how assets and responsibilities will be divided if you decide to end the partnership. The more specific the plan, the less chance there is for conflict.

6. Discuss money openly and regularly.

Don't put off talking about finances "until later." Hold monthly meetings or conference calls to review financial indicators and plan future investments.

7. Involve a lawyer from the beginning.

Even if you are sure that the terms are clear to both parties, a legal review of the contract will help you avoid ambiguities and loopholes in the wording.

Important: These recommendations are based on my personal experience working with partnership projects. I am not a lawyer, so be sure to consult with one who is familiar with your niche and jurisdiction before signing a contract.

Financial models and legal agreements form the foundation of a successful partnership project. Clear calculations, transparent distribution of profits and expenses, and written agreements allow you to plan your income and minimize conflicts.

We have broken down the process of building a financial model, from calculating expenses and distributing profits to accounting for non-financial contributions to the project. It is important to record not only money, but also the time, skills, and effort that each party contributes. This provides a clear picture of why a particular percentage ratio has been chosen and what each party receives in return.

The legal aspect helps secure these agreements and protect the project. A contract is not a formality; it's a tool that determines ownership of rights, income distribution, and what will happen if someone leaves the project. Analyzing practical mistakes and failure stories has shown that verbal promises, even between good acquaintances, do not guarantee security.

The main idea of this chapter is simple: a clear financial model plus legal documentation equals predictability and security. With these two tools, you can focus on developing and scaling your business rather than dealing with disputes and misunderstandings.

PART 3

CASE STUDIES AND VARIATIONS

CHAPTER 9

APPLYING THE MODEL TO EDUCATIONAL PRODUCTS

The profit-sharing model is not limited to traditional businesses. It is ideally suited to the educational products market, where profits are often distributed among several key players.

Online schools, courses, mentoring programs, and individual experts face the same challenges as large projects: how to divide revenue fairly, define responsibilities, and maintain partnerships as the business grows or changes.

In this chapter, we will explore how to adapt the model to different types of educational projects, ranging from large-scale schools to individual coaching practices. You will learn which nuances to consider in each case to avoid conflicts, accelerate growth, and maintain transparency.

This material is based on my personal experience and case studies of clients who have applied the model to real launches and long-term partnerships. This is not legal advice—I always recommend consulting lawyers when drafting contracts—but it is a distillation of practical solutions that have worked in real projects.

We will go through three key scenarios:

Online schools: When you have a team, several products, and a steady stream of sales.

Second, online courses, mentoring, and group programs, when the project is smaller but still has significant turnover.

The third scenario is individual experts, when the partnership is built around one person and their personal brand.

This chapter is about turning a partnership into a clear and predictable system where everyone knows their responsibilities and what they will receive in return.

Online Schools and the Profit Sharing Model

An online school is not just a single course or a one-time mentoring program. Rather, it is a full-fledged educational ecosystem in which several products can work simultaneously, including basic training programs, advanced courses, mentoring tracks, workshops, and highly specialized intensives. Unlike individual experts, an online school is built on a team model with clear roles, including marketing, sales, methodology, curatorial support, technical support, and operational management.

From a business perspective, an online school provides a steady stream of sales and content. Success depends not only on the charisma of the expert but also on the coordinated work of the entire team. Products within the school are often interconnected. For example, a basic course may lead a client to a more expensive program, while mentoring or a club can retain and increase lifetime value (LTV).

The Profit Sharing Model is particularly relevant for online schools

In the classic model, school owners pay their employees either a fixed salary or on a project basis. However, in a rapidly changing education market, this creates the risk of losing key people, as it becomes more profitable for them to leave for their own projects or competitors.

The profit sharing model solves this problem by aligning the interests of key team members with the school's revenue growth. When marketers, producers, experts, and operations managers understand that their income depends on the school's overall profit, their approach to work changes. Everyone starts thinking about long-term results rather than just "clocking in."

Additionally, online schools often have several product lines. Profit sharing allows you to:

- Transparently distribute profits between products and teams. For instance, a marketer could receive a share of all courses, while a methodologist only receives a share from the courses they teach.

- You can scale flexibly. You can add new products and areas without rethinking the entire financial system.

- Maintain motivation at every level. Even if a product is currently less profitable, the team knows that overall portfolio growth affects their income.

Learn how to structure roles, shares, and calculations in online schools.

1. Define key roles

There are two layers of the team in an online school:

- The strategic layer consists of people who influence the growth of the entire school, such as the owner/founder, producer, chief marketing officer, and chief methodologist. Their contribution is reflected in the results of all products.

- The product layer consists of teams responsible for specific courses or areas, such as curators, copywriters, designers, and technical support.

In the profit sharing model, it is often beneficial to separate the strategic layer's percentage from the percentage pool divided among the product teams.

Example:

- Strategic pool: 20% of the school's total net profit.

- Product pool: 30% of the profit from each product (divided among those involved).

- The remainder goes toward operating expenses and the business development fund.

2. Logic of Share Distribution

To avoid disputes, the following must be determined in advance:

- Fixed roles — the percentage does not depend on how many hours a person has worked. For example, 10% for the chief marketing officer and 5% for the chief methodologist.

- For flexible roles, the percentage is calculated using a formula linked to indicators, such as the number of leads attracted, lifetime value (LTV), or conversion rate.

Formula for flexible roles:

% = (specialist's result/target indicator) × set share.

Example:

If a targetologist is allocated up to 8% of the profit from the course and they bring in 80% of the target number of leads, their share is 6.4% (8% × 0.8).

3. Financial transparency

In online schools, it is especially important that the calculation of shares is transparent. To achieve this:

- Send a report on income and expenses once a month or after each launch (it can be in Google Sheets or CRM).

- All participants should see the same profit calculation formula to avoid different interpretations.

- If there are several products, assign a separate income/expense card to each one, and then sum everything up for the strategic pool.

4. Example of distribution in a real school

Revenue: $200,000 per month from several courses.

Expenses: $80,000 (advertising, salaries of employees not receiving shares, services). Net profit: $120,000.

1. Strategic pool (20%): $24,000.

- The producer receives 10% of the school's profits, or $12,000.

- Chief Marketing Officer:5% ($6,000)

- Chief Methodologist: 5% ($6,000)

2. Product pool: 30% of profits from each product

If a course generates $50,000 in net profit, the product team divides $15,000 among themselves.

- Curator: 5% ($2,500)

- Designer: 3% ($1,500)

- Technical Specialist: 2% ($1,000)

- Copywriter: 2% ($1,000)

- The remainder goes toward team bonuses.

5. How to Avoid Conflicts

- Put everything in writing, even if the team works on trust.

- Specify payment dates (e.g., by the 10th of the month).

- Discuss the mechanism for revising shares (e.g., if roles change or new tasks are added).

- Provide a monthly briefing on results so that everyone can see the connection between their contribution and the profit.

Applying the profit sharing model to online courses and mentoring programs

1. ures of this product category

Unlike online schools, where there is a constant flow of sales and several parallel projects, courses and mentoring programs often run in batches a group recruitment format on a specific date. Sales come in waves, and revenue and team workload depend on the launch cycle.

In this model:

- It is clear who did what and how much, and you can allocate percentages to specific launches.

- The team may change from launch to launch.

- It is easier to link shares to the results of a specific launch rather than to the results of the entire company.

2. Here's how to calculate percentages at launch:

The formula is often simpler than in online schools.

- First, take the net profit of the launch (revenue minus direct expenses, such as advertising, contractors, platforms, and taxes).

- Determine the total pool for the team (e.g., 30–40%).

- Divide it between roles.

Example:

Revenue from launching the mentoring program: $50,000.

Expenses: $15,000 (advertising: $10,000; contractors: $3,000; services: $2,000). Net profit: $35,000.

The team pool is 30%, or $10,500.

Producer: 12% ($4,200)

Marketer: 8% ($2,800)

Copywriter: 5% ($1,750)

Designer: 3% ($1,050)

Assistant: 2% ($700)

3. Flexibility of the model:

The advantage of profit sharing is that payments can be linked to specific tasks.

For example:

- If a marketer is responsible for both advertising and sales funnels, their percentage can be increased.

- If someone joins in the middle of a launch, they can receive a proportional share.

- Payments can be split into a fixed amount plus a percentage, so participants receive a minimum guarantee.

4. This model is particularly advantageous when:

- It is useful for small start-ups with limited budgets, when it is not possible to pay high fixed salaries.

- It is also advantageous for those who have a strong belief in the product and are willing to work for a percentage, understanding that the launch can generate high income.

- This model is also ideal for seasonal or one-off projects, such as marathons, challenges, and webinars.

5. Potential risks:

- If the launch is unsuccessful, the team will receive less than expected. This risk should be discussed honestly in advance.

- If profits increase significantly, the expert may want a smaller share next time, so it's important to set the percentages for several launches in advance.

- Without transparent expense reports, trust can easily be lost.

How does the Profit Sharing Model apply to individual experts and freelance specialists

1. Who does this apply to?

This category includes:

- Experts working under their own brand, such as coaches, consultants, trainers, and speakers.

- Freelancers with narrow expertise, such as marketers, designers, targetologists, copywriters, and developers.

- Specialists who run projects under their own name and find clients independently.

These specialists often do not have a large team or permanent office; they work with contractors, assistants, or other freelancers on a project basis.

2. What does profit sharing look like for them?

For individual experts, the model is built around project collaborations. For example:

- A coach might collaborate with an SMM specialist and receive a percentage of the sales from consultations.

- A designer agrees with a sales manager to receive a percentage of closed deals.

- A freelancer connects other freelancers to a project and distributes a percentage of the total profit.

The main idea is to avoid paying a fixed amount upfront and instead share the income from the results.

3. Calculation example

An expert offers a personal intensive course for $500 and sells 20 spots in a month.

Total revenue: $10,000. Expenses:

- Advertising: $1,500

- SMM specialist: 10% of sales ($1,000)

- Assistant: $500 fixed

Net profit: $7,000.

Instead of receiving the entire revenue, you can arrange for the SMM specialist to receive a percentage of the profit, or you can introduce a mixed model (fixed + percentage).

4. Why it works

- There is less risk for the expert because they don't spend a lot of money at the start.

- It motivates contractors because the percentage is directly linked to the result.

- It's an easy start to collaborations because it's easier to attract a specialist when you don't have to pay right away.

5. Potential challenges:

- If sales don't take off, the partner receives less or nothing, so it's important to discuss this in advance.

- There may be a temptation to "cut" the percentage after a successful launch, so it's best to fix the terms for several projects in advance.

- Keep transparent records of income and expenses to avoid conflicts.

6. Keys to success

- Always sign a written contract or agreement, even if it's simple.

- Make clear calculations and regularly report on the results.

- Agree on clear terms, including the percentage, payment terms, and the responsibilities of each party.

The profit sharing model has proven to be flexible enough to adapt to different formats of educational and expert projects, ranging from large-scale online schools to small personal brands and freelance practices.

With this model, online schools can grow without the excessive fixed salary costs of a large team. When specialists work for a percentage of the profit, the financial burden of launching new areas is reduced, and the team is highly motivated to deliver results.

Courses, mentoring programs, and author formats benefit from the ability to quickly assemble a team for a specific launch. The key advantage is the ability to bring together strong specialists without large investments by agreeing on a percentage of sales while testing different product formats.

Individual experts and freelancers can use the model to form collaborations where each partner contributes time, skills, and money. This opens the door to more ambitious projects than could be achieved alone.

The principle of shared responsibility and mutual benefit unites all three categories. The model helps optimize costs and creates a team atmosphere in which each participant is invested in the success of the common cause.

However, it is important to remember that such a system requires:

- Transparent accounting of income and expenses.

- Clearly defined agreements;

- An understanding that a percentage of profits is the main form of remuneration, not a "bonus on top."

With the right approach, the profit sharing model becomes a strategic tool for growth and retaining key partners in the project, not just a way to save money.

CHAPTER 10

APPLICATION OF THE PROFIT SHARING
MODEL IN TRADITIONAL BUSINESS

Although the Profit Sharing Model has already proven its effectiveness in online education, its potential is not limited to this field. In practice, the model can be successfully implemented in offline businesses, creative agencies, and service companies. It helps optimize costs, increase team engagement, and accelerate growth.

The main difference when applying the model to traditional businesses is that they often already have established operational processes, fixed costs, and a habit of paying employees fixed salaries. Switching to a percentage of profits requires a shift in thinking, but in exchange, businesses get teams focused on results rather than "clocking in."

In this chapter, we will discuss:

1. Offline businesses, such as cafes, coffee shops, beauty salons, and yoga studios, where the model can be integrated into the team's work.

2. Media and creative agencies, including projects in content, social media marketing (SMM), public relations (PR), design, and marketing.

3. Service companies, including repair, cleaning, consulting, tourism, event planning, and other types of services.

We will examine how to adapt the Profit Sharing Model to each segment and explore the associated advantages and pitfalls, providing practical examples.

In offline businesses such as coffee shops, restaurants, beauty salons, fitness studios, spas, and workshops, the profit sharing model can be an effective tool for both the internal team and external partners.

One effective option is to work with a marketer or business consultant on a profit-sharing basis.

Rather than paying a fixed fee for advertising or consulting services, the business owner pays the partner a percentage of the actual net profit earned above the base level. This incentivizes them to increase revenue and allows business owners to pay for actual results rather than promises.

Why is the percentage lower offline than online?

Offline businesses have higher fixed costs, such as rent, utilities, salaries, and purchases of materials and equipment. The net profit from which the partner's percentage is paid is lower than that of digital projects, where scaling is cheaper.

Therefore, the distribution for a marketer or consultant is most often 5–20% of the additional net profit rather than the total revenue.

This is how it works in practice:

First, we determine the baseline: how much the business was earning before working with the partner.

Then, we calculate the increase by measuring how much profit came in above the base level on a monthly or quarterly basis.

Then, we divide the profit by fixing the percentage that the marketer or consultant receives from the increase.

Finally, we set the terms. The contract must specify the calculation formula, data sources, and payment terms.

Example:

Before the partnership, a beauty salon earned $8,000 in net profit per month. After launching a marketing campaign and optimizing processes, profits grew to $12,000.

The increase was $4,000.

According to the contract, the marketer receives 15% of the increase, or $600.

Thus, rather than paying for work, the owner pays for real results, and the marketer is directly motivated to increase profits.

Advantages for offline businesses:

- Flexibility: The business does not incur unnecessary expenses during slow months.

- The consultant focuses on results, not beautiful presentations.

- Mutually beneficial partnership: Both parties are interested in long-term growth.

What to look for:

- Transparent accounting: All figures must be confirmed by the accounting department or CRM.

- A clear distinction of influence is important. If other factors contribute to growth, such as renovation, a new product, or a season, it is important to specify how this affects payments.

- Contract terms: It is often advantageous to sign a three- to six-month contract with the option to extend.

Application of the profit sharing model in media businesses and social media marketing (SMM): A business consultant and marketer's perspective

As a consultant and marketer, I often see media businesses — from SMM studios to production teams and PR agencies — underestimate the potential of the Profit Sharing Model. At the same time, it is precisely in this area that the model is not just "suitable," but it can also transform the way businesses interact with clients and take projects to a strategic level.

That's why I recommend the model for media and SMM.

Traditional payment methods, such as a fixed monthly fee, a package of posts, or an advertising budget, rarely provide clients with a sense of guaranteed results. This is one reason why marketing often works on short contracts.

Businesses want to quickly assess the outcome and switch contractors at the slightest sign of doubt.

Profit sharing removes this barrier. Instead of paying for posts, layouts, or hours of work, clients pay for measurable increases in sales, leads, or profits. In my experience, this has led even large companies to be more willing to launch a trial collaboration because their risks are minimal.

How to calculate and set terms

In the media business, we have a unique advantage because we can directly influence our clients' revenue through digital channels where ROI and analytics are transparent.

Depending on the niche, I set a profit-sharing percentage between 15% and 40%.

Important points to consider when working together:

1. Success metrics: We set specific KPIs, such as revenue growth, number of orders, and customer acquisition cost.

2. A comparative base: I always ask for data from previous periods to accurately track the effect.

3. Access to analytics, such as CRM, advertising accounts, and web analytics, is necessary for an honest calculation.

4. The trial period is usually 3–6 months, after which the terms can be revised.

For example, an SMM agency I worked with as a consultant took on an online accessories store.

An SMM agency that I consulted for took on an online accessories store. Before we started working together, the client received 120 orders per month, with an average order value of $60 and a margin of 35%.

We implemented a content marketing strategy with bloggers, optimized the target audience, and added an email funnel.

After three months, there were 230 orders. Increase: $110 \times \$60 \times 35\% = \$2,310$ in additional profit. According to the contract, the agency received 30% — $693 per month in commission alone, plus a fixed fee for basic work.

There are advantages for marketers and consultants

- It is easier to approach new clients with a "no risk" offer than with just a price list for services.

- Higher check size due to results — if you improve the metrics significantly, the client is willing to pay more.

- Long-term contracts — businesses don't want to lose their partner when the model works.

Risks and how I mitigate them:

- Dependence on the client: Problems with the product, logistics, or service can ruin the result. Solution: At the beginning, I analyze the client's business model and provide recommendations on how to eliminate weak points.

- Complex calculations: Sometimes, CRM refinement or tracking implementation is required. I include this as a mandatory stage of model implementation.

- Deferred income: Profits may not be immediately apparent. I often combine a percentage with a minimum fixed fee to cover the team's basic expenses.

Application of the Profit Sharing Model in Service Companies

When working with service companies, such as repair services, cleaning services, IT support, and logistics operators, B2B consulting—I see the same pattern: marketing is often perceived as an "expense" rather than an "investment." Clients are used to paying a fixed amount for advertising or promotion without considering what percentage of that amount actually turns into profit.

The Profit Sharing Model changes this paradigm. Instead of coming to a business with a price list for hours or banners, I come with an offer: "You only pay me for profit growth or an increase in orders." This reduces initial resistance and increases trust — the business understands that I only earn money when it does.

This model works especially well in service industries.

Services always involve repeat sales, word-of-mouth advertising, and long-term customer relationships. The value of one attracted customer is higher here than in one-time retail sales. For instance, if I help a dentist attract a patient for a $100 cleaning, that patient may return for a $2,000 implant or refer the clinic to friends.

In such cases, profit sharing motivates me to build marketing strategies that focus not only on quick deals but also on establishing a long-term customer base, which benefits both parties.

Here's how I work with calculations in service businesses

Unlike e-commerce or media, where results are visible the next day, the transaction cycle in services can be longer. Therefore, I often use a hybrid model of a minimum fixed fee to cover my expenses plus a percentage of each sale or revenue increase.

Example structure:

- Fixed fee: $1,000 per month to cover operating costs.

- 20–30% of the additional profit or paid orders that come through my channels.

The success metrics for such projects are the number of leads, conversion to payment, and customer lifetime value (LTV). I always spell this out in the contract so that the calculations are transparent.

Example from my practice:

I consulted with a small chain of massage parlors. Before we started working together, they had 180 appointments per month. We implemented a lead magnet system via Instagram, set up audience targeting by radius, and created a referral program.

After two months, they had 250 appointments. The average check was $75, with a margin of ~50%. Increase: 70%× $75 × 50% = $2,625. My 25% commission was an additional $656 per month on top of my fixed salary.

There are advantages for me as a consultant and marketer

- I was able to quickly enter the business. When the owner heard that I was willing to share the risk and income, I stood out from those who just sold "Marketing for a price."

- Long-term relationships: Businesses rarely change marketers if they see growth.

- Unlimited income growth: The better my strategies work, the higher my percentage.

Risks and how I mitigate them:

- Seasonality of demand: Some services experience pronounced peaks and troughs. I predict these in advance and build campaigns that take seasonal fluctuations into account.

- Dependence on service quality: Even the best marketing won't save you if the services are poor. That's why I always include a service audit and recommendations for improvement.

- Uneven cash flow: Payment from clients may come later in services. The solution is a fixed fee plus a clear payment schedule.

The profit sharing model in offline and service businesses is not just a new payment format; it's also a way to change the mindset of company owners and marketers. Rather than viewing promotion as a fixed expense, businesses begin to perceive it as a partnership where both parties are interested in the same result: profit growth.

This model creates unique conditions for coffee shops, salons, studios, media companies, SMM agencies, and service providers: the marketer or business consultant becomes a full-fledged participant in the process, not an external contractor. They are involved in strategy, product quality, customer service, and audience retention because every improvement directly affects their income.

While the profit distribution percentage is usually lower in offline businesses than in online businesses, there is another advantage here: stability. A steady stream of customers, repeat sales, and location loyalty provide predictability and the opportunity to build long-term relationships. The potential is even higher in media and service companies because digital metrics allow you to quickly track results and adjust your strategy.

As a result, applying the Profit Sharing Model to these niches creates a situation in which marketing ceases to be an expense and becomes an asset that generates measurable, mutually beneficial results. This builds trust, retains customers for years, and gives consultants the opportunity to increase their income without a hard ceiling.

CHAPTER 11

MISTAKES AND PITFALLS

When the Profit Sharing Model Doesn't Work

Although the profit-sharing model opens up enormous opportunities, there are situations in which it is ineffective or doomed to fail from the beginning. It is crucial for marketers and consultants to recognize these conditions before signing a contract and investing their efforts.

1. Lack of a product or service ready for sale

If the client does not have a finished product, service, or even a minimum viable product (MVP), your work as a marketer will focus on refinement and testing rather than sales. In such cases:

- Time is spent on development and packaging, but the profit from which you are supposed to receive a percentage simply does not exist.

- The product may never make it to market.

In conclusion, the model works when there is something to sell from the first month. If the product is "in the process of being created," request a resolution or postpone the start of your collaboration.

2. Disagreement on goals and values

If you and your client have different ideas about strategy, pace of development, and approaches to promotion, conflict is inevitable. For example:

- You are planning a long-term strategy involving warm-ups and funnel building, while the client expects "instant" profits overnight.

- You prefer ethical promotion, but the client is willing to use aggressive spam.

Conclusion: From the beginning, determine whether your values, approaches, and expectations are aligned.

3. Financial opacity

In the profit sharing model, your profit depends on the client's honesty. If there is no transparent accounting system and the revenue data is "somewhere in the accountant's spreadsheet" and you are not shown it, you are at risk.

- You have no access to CRM or analytics.

- Revenue is recorded as "cash" or on personal cards.

- Clients "forget" about some sales.

In conclusion, do not enter into a transaction without transparent reporting and access to figures.

4. Lack of customer readiness for change

Sometimes, clients want growth but are not ready to implement recommendations.

- They don't improve a weak offer, even if it hinders sales.

- They refuse to create content, adjust prices, or improve service.

Conclusion: If the client is unwilling to invest effort in improving the product, your work will not yield results, and you will be left without income.

5. Poor Reputation or Toxic Product

Even the best marketing won't save you if the product is bad or has a questionable reputation. Example:

- Cosmetics with fake certificates.

- An online course that received negative reviews.

In conclusion, assess the reputation of the client and the product before associating your name with them.

6. Unrealistic expectations regarding deadlines and scope of work.

If a client expects you to "double their revenue in a month" with zero investment and perform sales, support, and logistics functions, — this is an alarm signal.

Conclusion: Define your responsibilities in the contract, and agree on realistic deadlines for achieving results.

Red flags at the start of a deal in a profit-sharing model

Experienced professionals know that even the most profitable project can fail if you ignore signs that your partner or expert is not the right person to share profits with. Below are key indicators that can help you identify a problematic deal in advance.

1. Unwillingness to disclose financial information:

- Refusal to show turnover, average checks, conversions, or the number of leads.

- They do not provide access to CRM, analytics, or advertising accounts.

- Everything is kept in a "notebook" or based on verbal agreements.

Why it's dangerous: You won't be able to adequately assess the deal's potential or calculate your share. This means you risk working "blind."

2. History of failed partnerships:

- They speak excessively negatively about former marketers or consultants.

- They blame past contractors for all problems without analyzing their own mistakes.

Why it's dangerous: There is a high probability that, in a couple of months, you will find yourself "at fault" in their eyes.

3. Vague goals and lack of strategy:

- They are unable to clearly explain why they want growth or what figures they want to achieve.

- They say things like "We sell everything to everyone" or "I just want more money," without any segmentation or understanding of the niche.

You'll constantly be putting out fires and changing course, losing time and efficiency.

4. Unwillingness to invest in growth.

- They expect marketing to be "free."

- They are not ready to invest in content, advertising, or product improvement.

Why it's dangerous: Without investment, it's impossible to scale up, and you'll end up with no profit.

5. Complex or toxic communication style:

- Ignores messages or responds once a week.

- Often changes decisions at the last minute.

- They use manipulation or passive aggression.

Why it's dangerous: Communicating with such a partner will require more effort than it will yield results.

6. Legal or reputational "gray area":

- A product with questionable certifications or ethical issues.

- There are negative reviews in open sources, but the client does not intend to work with them.

Why it's dangerous: You could lose your reputation by being associated with a problematic brand.

7. They have unrealistic expectations regarding deadlines.

- They require "doubling sales in a month" without a customer base or investment.

- It does not take into account seasonality or actual transaction cycles.

Why it's dangerous: There is a high risk that the project will be deemed "unsuccessful" long before any results can be achieved.

8. There is no business structure.

- There is no manager or person responsible for implementing your ideas.

- All processes are chaotic, and decisions are made only by the owner with delays.

Why it's dangerous: Your strategies will get stuck at the implementation stage.

Entering into a partnership or launching "on trust" is risky. Even the most charismatic expert or partner may turn out to be unsuitable if warning signs are ignored at the outset. Step-by-step diagnostics help you identify potential problems in advance and determine whether it's worth delving deeper into the work or if it's better to stop. This approach saves time, money, and stress while increasing the likelihood of building a project on honest and transparent terms.

Conduct step-by-step diagnostics before entering into a deal.

1. First impression

Pay attention to how quickly and willingly the person responds.

Do they avoid answering simple questions or delay correspondence and calls?

This may be a sign that communication will be difficult in the future.

2. Transparency of information

Is your partner willing to show you their current results, such as turnover, funnels, coverage, and past launches?

If they hide data under the pretext of "not ready yet" or "don't want to show," it's a strong signal to pause.

3. Willingness to discuss terms

Is the partner willing to talk honestly about profit sharing and each party's contributions?

If they keep saying, "Let's discuss it later," or "We'll figure it out as we go," there is a high probability of conflict.

4. Realistic goals

Requests such as "I want x10 per month with no budget or team" indicate mismatched expectations.

Ask whether the person understands that results require time, testing, and investment.

5. Check values and work style

Are your approaches to customers, products, and advertising aligned?

Conflicting values almost always lead to deals falling through.

6. Mini Cooperation Test

Before signing an agreement, conduct a small test. Give your partner a task or agree on a trial period.

Observe how they respond to deadlines, feedback, and teamwork.

7. Financial discipline

How does your partner feel about money? Do they keep records? Are they willing to put agreements in writing?

If everything is verbal and unconfirmed, the risks are high.

How to get out of a deal if the project stopped working

Even with excellent preparation and motivation, there are situations when a project stops delivering results. Reasons can include personal conflicts, burnout, and sudden market changes. It's important to end the collaboration in a timely and competent manner to minimize losses and preserve your reputation.

1. Treat withdrawal as a management decision.

The end of a project is not necessarily a failure, but rather a natural conclusion to a phase. Approach the decision without emotion. Assess the situation, document everything, and close any outstanding commitments.

2. Define the "exit point" in advance.

The foundation for a smooth parting is laid in the contract. Specify the conditions under which each party can terminate cooperation, such as failure to meet KPIs or delays in providing materials. Writing it down turns a potential conflict into routine agreement fulfillment.

3. Check if the situation can be remedied.

Before making a final decision, ask yourself the following questions:

- Has everything been done to resolve the issue?

- Does the partner understand the situation?

- Is it really more profitable to exit now than to continue?

Often, the problem lies in communication, not the business model. Sometimes, clarifying expectations and removing barriers is all it takes for the project to get back on track.

4. Ensure transparent communication.

There should be no "disappearances" or abrupt breaks. Organize a meeting or conference call to explain the reasons and propose a smooth exit plan.

- Complete current tasks.

- Transfer all materials and access.

- Set clear dates and agree on a financial settlement.

    The more specific the terms, the lower the risk of future conflicts.

5. Consider a compromise.

If the project has value, reduce it to the bare minimum: monthly consultations, for example.

6. Maintain your reputation.

Even if your partner behaves incorrectly, avoid public accusations. In a professional manner, document your claims in writing. In public communications, simply announce the termination of the partnership.

    Sometimes, it is worth offering a bonus or accepting the partner's work without additional conditions. This increases the likelihood that they will recommend you.

7. Act in a timely manner.

Exiting at an early stage when it's clear the model isn't working is a sign of maturity, not de. The experience gained will help you quickly recognize "red flags" in the future.

    In summary, this chapter on mistakes and pitfalls in working with the Profit Sharing Model can be boiled down to several key conclusions.

First, the success of a deal is determined before it even starts. During the negotiation and partner evaluation stage, you must be attentive: review the numbers, check past results, observe behavior, and assess willingness to share information. Any "red flag," from an unwillingness to show real metrics to constantly postponing meetings, is a signal that you should either dig deeper or walk away.

Second, project diagnostics are not a formality but a tool for self-defense. Even a simple, step-by-step check will help you determine if it's worth investing your time and expertise. It's important to evaluate not only the product and niche but also the partners themselves, including their motivation, stress tolerance, teamwork skills, and ability to accept feedback.

Third, knowing when to walk away from a deal is a sign of professionalism, not de. The sooner you admit a project is not going in the right direction, the less you will lose. At the same time, it is important to exit correctly. Record agreements in writing and settle financial issues to preserve your reputation and the opportunity to work with this person or their circle in the future.

The main idea of this chapter is simple: the profit-sharing model can be profitable and promising, but only with careful partner selection, honest expectations on both sides, and a willingness to make quick decisions when reality does not match the plan. A professional protects not only the client's interests but also their own resources—time, energy, and reputation.

PART 4

STANDARDIZATION AND SCALING

CHAPTER 12

METHODOLOGY AS A SYSTEM

WHAT MAKES THE PROFIT SHARING LAUNCH MODEL A SYSTEM

A successful methodology is more than just a set of ideas and tips that "kind of work." Rather, it is a clear system that can be replicated with predictable results, regardless of who applies it: you, your partner, or your team. The Profit Sharing Launch Model was created with this goal in mind: to transform chaotic launches into a scalable, adaptable, and transferable mechanism.

1. The model is composed of clearly defined stages.

At the heart of the model is a structure broken down into stages, each with its own goal, set of tasks, and success criteria. There are no vague concepts such as "prepare a little" or "launch the ad somehow." Rather, there is a step-by-step roadmap, from product diagnosis and packaging to closing sales and analyzing results. Each stage is linked to the previous one and logically flows into the next, like a well-designed assembly line.

2. The logic of transitioning between stages

One of the main advantages of the system is its clear logic about when and under what conditions you can move forward. In chaotic launches, it is common for the team to jump to sales without preparation or launch advertising without testing the offer. In the Profit Sharing Launch Model, such "jumps" are impossible; you can only move forward after completing specific checkpoints. This doesn't slow things down. Instead, it saves time and money by avoiding actions that are bound to fail.

3. **The system is reusable without loss of quality.**

The system was designed so that it can be used repeatedly without reinventing the wheel. Of course, there are nuances of adaptation for each niche and audience, but the core elements—structure, sequence, and key tools—remain the same. This is especially important for producers and consultants who manage multiple projects because they can copy and scale processes instead of building them from scratch every time.

4. **Link to measurable results.**

The model leaves no room for subjective "it seems to have worked." Each stage is linked to KPIs, such as reach, conversion to application, cost per lead, average check, and deal duration. This allows you to identify issues early on and make adjustments before the budget is exhausted or the audience becomes overwhelmed. This transforms the methodology from a "black box" into a manageable tool.

5. **Supporting tools.**

The system is not just a concept; it is a set of ready-made materials:

Checklists, scripts, content templates, sample commercial proposals, contract templates, and task planners. These materials enable you to quickly onboard new team members, train partners, and maintain consistent quality standards.

Bottom line: The Profit Sharing Launch Model is more than just a "launch methodology." It is a complete operating system for online sales where every element is subject to a common logic, making the result reproducible and predictable. With this approach, launching becomes a manageable business process, not a lottery.

Learn how to integrate the model into your consulting practice.

The Profit Sharing Launch Model is not just a separate launch methodology. It is a holistic approach that can become the core of your consulting practice. It will change your client strategy, financial model, reputation, and scope of influence.

Integrating the model transforms disparate projects into a structured system, ensuring that each launch is a step toward predictable results.

1. Understanding the value of the model is key.

Before implementing the model in your practice, it is important to deeply understand its value.

- Financial flexibility: You earn fixed fees and a percentage of the results.

- Long-term partnerships: Working with this model means you are interested in your clients' success. This type of collaboration is built on trust and mutual benefit.

- Access to larger deals: Unlike one-off consultations, the model allows you to participate in larger projects and influence your clients' overall business growth.

This understanding is critical. When you are confident that the model benefits both parties, it is easier to argue its value in negotiations and position yourself correctly.

2. Choosing the right clients is also important.

Not every project is suitable for profit sharing. For integration to be successful, it is important to select clients who:

- Have growth and scaling potential.

- The client's product or service already has proven demand, even if only on a small scale.

- The client is ready for transparency regarding figures and understands the need to invest in marketing and launch preparation.

Initially, select 2–3 clients who best meet these criteria and develop pilot cases with them. These cases will form the foundation for scaling the model across your entire practice.

3. Restructure the work process.

For the model to work, you must change the structure of your interactions with clients.

- Conduct clear diagnostics before launching. Instead of jumping straight into launching, start by analyzing your audience, product, promotional channels, and previous results.

- Create a launch roadmap so the client has a clear understanding of the stages that will be completed, from warm-up to post-launch analysis.

- Implement a KPI and control point system. Record key metrics (e.g., leads, conversions, and sales) and agree on them in advance so both parties understand what constitutes a "successful result."

4. Financial model and legal framework

Profit sharing requires a special approach to agreements.

- Use a transparent profit calculation formula that clearly defines what counts as profit and when it is divided.

- Include an agreement with exit terms that specifies how the parties can terminate cooperation if the project does not deliver results or if agreements are violated.

- Offer flexible payment options. Sometimes, you can combine a fixed fee and a percentage to provide a basic income guarantee while showing the client that you are motivated to achieve results.

5. Tools, templates, and automation

Once you have implemented the model, minimize manual routine tasks.

- Create a client brief template to quickly gather key information.

- Develop a launch checklist for the team so that everyone knows their scope of work and deadlines.

- Set up an analytics system (e.g., Google Data Studio, Airtable, or Notion) to track progress in real time.

These changes will speed up processes and increase client trust because they will see that you work according to a system, not "by feel."

6. Impact on revenue and business growth

Integrating the Profit Sharing Launch Model can radically change your financial dynamics.

- Even one successful client can generate several times more revenue each month than a one-time consultation.

- A portfolio of three to five such clients creates a stable stream of high-margin income.

- You can then gradually move away from small, unprofitable orders to focus on projects that deliver meaningful results.

It's important to understand that the model requires more involvement initially, but over time, especially with a system and team in place, it scales without a proportional increase in workload.

7. Scaling within the practice

Once you have tested the model on your first cases, you can:

- Train your team to handle part of the process without your direct involvement.

- Delegate content preparation, advertising, and analytics.

- Create a product line. For example, in addition to a full launch, you could offer clients strategic sessions, funnel audits, and warm-up reviews.

This way, the model ceases to be a "manual project" and becomes a replicable system.

Metrics and quality control

Why it's important:

In the Profit Sharing Launch Model, we must manage results with equal precision for online launches and offline sales. While online projects' figures are immediately visible in analytics, offline businesses need to manually build a measurement system or use CRM/POS software.

What to measure:

1.   Warm-up and attraction

Online: Stories reach, email CTR, landing page conversion, and lead cost.

Offline: number of visits to the point of sale, responses to advertising, calls/requests, and average cost per customer acquired.

2.   Sales:

Online: conversion of requests into payments, upselling, and returns.

Offline: average check, sales from promotions, and upsells at checkout.

3.   Retention:

Online: percentage of repeat purchases, community activity, and newsletter subscriptions.

Offline: Customer returns via bonus cards, loyalty programs, and reviews.

4.   Response speed:

Online: response time via messenger and email.

Offline: speed of service in the store or over the phone and feedback on complaints.

How to implement monitoring:

Online: Google Analytics, CRM, and automatic reports.

For offline, use CRM with visit tracking, POS reports, and tables with daily measurements.

In both cases, there should be weekly "number crunching" and strategy adjustments.

How to transfer the model to the team:

Simply giving instructions is not enough to transfer the Profit Sharing Launch Model to the team. It is a process in which preserving the model's philosophy is important, including its approach to distributing responsibility, focusing on results, and ensuring process transparency.

1. The foundation is a single source of truth

The first thing you need to create is a single knowledge base. This can be:

- an online platform (Notion, Confluence, or a Trello board with checklists);

- a local database with a clear folder structure (Google Drive);

- for offline businesses, it can be a hybrid system (printed instructions + electronic version).

This database should include:

- Model documentation, from philosophy to step-by-step processes;

- Checklists and templates for presentations, scripts, letters, and advertising materials.

- Case studies with real results;

- An FAQ library for new team members.

These resources will enable every employee, whether a sales manager in a brick-and-mortar store or a target specialist at an online school, to understand exactly how the model works and what steps are required.

2. Step-by-step training

Don't expect the team to "figure it out on their own," even with perfect documentation. You need to build a training structure.

Start with an overview session to show the entire model, including its principles, stages, and roles, as well as how profit is calculated.

In-depth modules by role: Training focused on specific tasks:

- For marketers, explain how to launch campaigns within the model.

- For project managers, explain how to monitor stage completion.

- For sales managers, it should cover how to get customers to pay.

Case study practice: Launch a test mini-project with real-life conditions.

Readiness assessment includes tests, error analysis, and corrections.

For offline businesses, this can take the form of on-site master classes (e.g., for store teams), while online businesses can take advantage of Zoom sessions with recording and access to a knowledge base.

3. Roles and areas of responsibility

For the model to work, the team must understand:

- Who is responsible for which stage.

- What metrics determine the success of the work;

- How tasks are transferred between participants.

Example:

The marketing department attracts leads within the budget.

The sales department converts leads into deals.

The operations manager monitors deadlines and coordinates changes.

The customer service department ensures retention and repeat purchases.

4. Quality Control

Model transfer is not a "one-and-done" process. A quality control system must be built in.

- Regular calls (weekly/monthly)
- Metrics reports (leads, conversion, ROI)
- Error analysis: What went wrong and how to fix it.
- Adjust templates based on experience.

Offline, this could be a planning meeting at the end of a shift or week. Online, it could be a sync via Zoom or Slack.

5. Feedback culture

The key to model sustainability is two-way communication. Team members should not be afraid to suggest improvements:

- Feedback form in the knowledge base.
- Regular surveys on the usability of templates and processes;
- Joint analysis of successful and unsuccessful cases

6. Gradually scale

Once the team is accustomed to the model:

- Launch more projects in parallel (online: different products; offline: new branches).

- Create internal "model ambassadors": experienced employees who train newcomers.

- Add new tools and channels to the model while preserving its core.

Transferring the Profit Sharing Launch Model is more than just training. It is establishing a system that functions independently and a team that comprehends the rationale behind each step. Once implemented and accepted across the organization, the model becomes self-sustaining and produces results even without the founder's involvement in every process.

Knowledge base and case library

Why is this necessary?

Online and offline teams often lose experience because it "stays in people's heads." A centralized database transforms every idea, script, and example into a reusable resource.

What to store:

- Detailed launch analyses (online and offline), including figures and context

- Sales scripts (chat, phone call, and face-to-face meeting)

- Photos/videos from events, storefronts, and advertising layouts.

- Templates for posts, stories, emails, and offline advertising (e.g., flyers and banners).

- Technical instructions: online — funnel setup; offline — window display design, venue preparation, and POS setup.

How to organize:

Online: Notion, Confluence, and Google Drive with tags and search functions.

Offline: same platforms, plus printed instructions at points of sale and QR access to materials.

Update after each launch or promotion to keep the database current. Result:

Reduce the time needed to prepare a new launch by 50–70%.

You will have the ability to quickly scale successful approaches across different locations or projects.

There is continuous improvement in the quality and consistency of results.

When we view the Profit Sharing Launch Model as a system rather than a set of separate steps, we see that its strength lies in the integration of all elements.

Each block we have discussed, from step-by-step implementation to transferring the model to the team, is not just a tool. Together, they create a sustainable business architecture in which:

- There is predictability (we know what to expect at every stage).

- Quality is maintained (metrics and controls prevent slippage), and efficiency increases (templates, checklists, and a case database save resources).

- efficiency increases (templates, checklists, and a case database save resources);

- Scaling occurs without losing the essence, and knowledge is transferred quickly and completely.

This system makes launches independent of mood or random ideas and dependent on clear logic and proven actions. This is especially critical for online businesses, where the pace of change is faster, and for offline projects, where mistakes are more costly.

It is precisely this complex combination of:

structure,

measurability,

reproducibility,

team interaction

that transforms the model from a working method into a strategic asset.

A system is not about rigid frameworks, but rather, it is about having freedom within a proven structure. With a clear framework, you can adapt it creatively to any niche and still guarantee results.

CHAPTER 13

THE FUTURE OF THE MODEL

How the Profit-Sharing Model Is Changing Consulting and Marketing

1. The Transition from Project to Partnership

Traditionally, consulting and marketing work is project-based. The client orders a service, the consultant or agency delivers it, and that's the end of the interaction. The PSM radically changes this logic. The consultant and marketer become strategic partners of the business, interested in its sustainable growth. The success of a campaign or implemented strategy directly affects both parties' income, improving the quality and depth of the work.

2. Alignment of interests and incentive for growth

With a fixed fee, a consultant or marketer may only be interested in completing the assigned tasks on time. In the PSM model, however, the motivation changes. An increase in the client's revenue means an increase in the specialist's income. This encourages them to seek not only quick solutions but also long-term scaling strategies.

3. High-level expertise becomes more accessible

Many small businesses and experts cannot afford expensive marketing agencies or experienced consultants at a fixed rate. PSM makes these services more accessible because the initial investment is minimal, and payment is based on actual growth. This opens access to high-quality strategies for those who previously had to work with less experienced specialists.

4. Applications are expanding beyond online business

Although the model has particularly well taken root in digital products, online courses, and e-commerce, it is increasingly being used by offline businesses— from beauty salons and clinics to restaurants and local services. In these niches, PSM allows for the implementation of marketing strategies without large initial costs, enabling growth for even small companies.

5. Standardization and quality improvement

Working on a percentage basis requires a systematic approach, including detailed analytics, clear KPIs, and transparent reporting. PSM consultants and marketers develop internal standards, templates, and methodologies that can be scaled and applied to different projects. This raises the overall level of professionalism in the market.

6. Strengthening trust and transparency

Since the outcome directly impacts both parties' income, the model fosters a culture of open finances and transparent data. This strengthens long-term relationships and minimizes misunderstandings often encountered in fixed payment schemes.

7. Development of a new type of specialist

Within the PSM, strategists who can see the big picture, analyze the market, and create sustainable growth models are valued as much as task performers. These specialists are in high demand, and the model itself contributes to their development.

Standardization of approach and methodology

At some point, every consultant or marketer working under the PSM faces the same challenge: project after project and client after client, the solutions become repetitive. Yes, there are nuances and unique tasks, but the structure of the actions is surprisingly similar.

It is at this moment that the idea arises: "What if I put this into a single system that will work even without my constant supervision?"

From chaos to algorithm:

Initially, the model exists only in your head as a set of successful phrases, techniques, and templates that have been tested in practice. However, as long as it remains an "oral tradition," the business remains vulnerable because much depends on your memory and involvement.

Standardization starts with a simple step: documentation. Every successful step, every calculated risk, and every repeatable result is recorded.

Gradually, the framework of the methodology emerges: stages, key actions, and control points. It is important at this point to transition from the idea of "doing everything from scratch every time" to the principle of "copying and adapting."

Methodology is the DNA of business

Once a process becomes repeatable, it transcends being merely a set of tools; it becomes the DNA of your work. Methodology provides a framework while allowing room for creativity. It works like a map;

145

anyone on the team or from partner companies can follow it without getting lost in the details.

This is especially important in the context of profit sharing: after all, profits are only shared when the project delivers results. Standardization reduces errors, speeds up launches, and provides clients with predictability.

From personal expertise to team strength

Methodology becomes valuable when others can use it. Three things are important here:

- Clarity: Any new team member understands what is being done and why.

- Transparency: Each stage has quality criteria and metrics.

- Scalability: The methodology can be applied to both online and offline businesses without significant modifications.

Thus, standardization is not about "freezing creativity," but rather, freeing it from routine to allow it to grow.

Transferring and scaling the methodology

Once you have developed and refined the Profit Sharing Model using your own cases, the next stage is to replicate it by training other specialists. This is not a byproduct, but a strategic part of the methodology itself. The model is designed to be reproducible without any loss of quality.

1. Standardization of the process

The methodology is documented in step-by-step modules with clear descriptions of the objectives of each step, the necessary tools, examples, checklists, control points, and success metrics. This transforms experience into an "algorithm" that can be transferred to any specialist, regardless of their background.

2. Training is based on methodological materials

The training program is designed so that participants understand the model's logic and can apply it to a real project. In the manual, this process is described as a "learning cycle":

- learning the theory,

- completing a practical assignment,

- analysis and correction,

- implementation in the work process.

3. Certification is an element of quality control.

To ensure the methodology's continued value, specialists undergo certification. This guarantees that everyone working according to the model adheres to standards, ensuring predictable results for clients.

4. The "train the trainers" model

Certified specialists can become mentors for new participants. This lays the foundation for exponential growth: The more trained mentors there are, the faster the model spreads.

5. The ecosystem effect

A community forms within the methodology where participants exchange new tools, case studies, and improvements. It's not just a network of specialists; it's a living system that evolves and keeps the methodology relevant.

CONCLUSION

In a world where customers expect more than just services — they expect tangible growth — the Profit Sharing Model is becoming more than just a way of working. It is a new philosophy of partnership.

For marketers and consultants, it is an opportunity to transition from being a "hired expert" to becoming a co-author of business success. Each new project becomes a story in which your decisions directly affect profits, not just a case study in your portfolio.

When working under a profit-sharing model, your focus changes. Instead of focusing on the hours worked and tasks completed, you focus on what will really bring growth to the client. There is a special satisfaction in seeing your strategies turn into real results and profits into income.

The Profit Sharing Model opens up financial opportunities and doors to projects that can change your career. One day, you could be a partner to a small business; the next, you could be part of a team bringing a brand to the national or international market.

Ultimately, this is a story not just about money, but also about influence. It's about how your experience and ideas can help companies grow, create jobs, set new standards, and advance entire industries.

Now is the time to stop selling your time and start investing your talent where it can bring you and the world the greatest return.

Link your success directly to your clients' success, and you will both grow without limits. That is the true power of the Profit Sharing Model.

www.ingramcontent.com/pod-product-compliance
Lightning Source LLC
Chambersburg PA
CBHW050642190326
41458CB00008B/2385